The FANTASTIC COSTUME BOOK

This book is dedicated to my mother, who has "gebentched hent."

Editing: Thom Boswell
Design and Production: Chris Colando
Photography: Evan Bracken

Library of Congress Cataloging-in-Publication Data

Lipson, Michelle.
    The fantastic costume book : 40 complete patterns to amaze and
amuse / by Michelle Lipson and friends ; [photography, Evan Bracken].
        p.   cm.
    "A Sterling/Lark book"--T.p. verso.
    Includes index.
    ISBN 0-8069-8376-0
    1. Costume.   2. Handicraft.   3. Children's clothing.   I. Title.
TT633.L57   1992
646.4'78--dc20   92-11365
                                              CIP

10 9 8 7 6 5 4 3 2

A Sterling/Lark Book

First paperback edition published in 1993 by
Sterling Publishing Company, Inc.
387 Park Avenue South, New York, N.Y. 10016

Produced by Altamont Press, Inc.
50 College Street, Asheville, NC 28801

© 1992, Altamont Press

Distributed in Canada by Sterling Publishing
℅ Canadian Manda Group, P.O. Box 920, Station U
Toronto, Ontario, Canada M8Z 5P9
Distributed in Great Britain and Europe by Cassell PLC
Villiers House, 41/47 Strand, London WC2N 5JE, England
Distributed in Australia by Capricorn Link Ltd.
P.O. Box 665, Lane Cove, NSW 2066

Every effort has been made to ensure that all the information in this book is accurate. However, due to differing conditions, tools, and individual skills, the publisher cannot be responsible for any injuries, losses, and other damages which may result from the use of the information in this book.

Sterling ISBN 0-8069-8376-0 Trade
          0-8069-8377-9 Paper

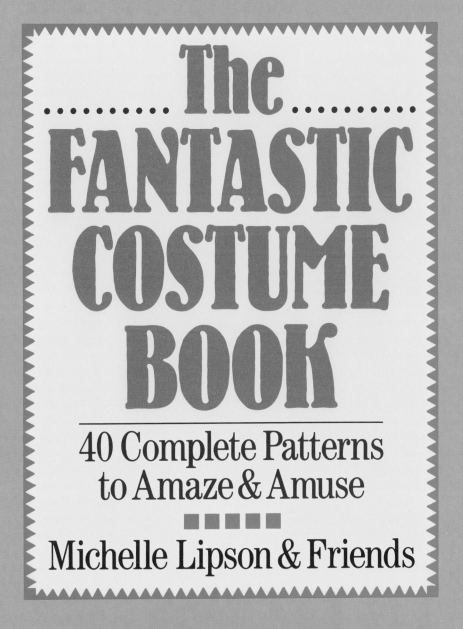

The
FANTASTIC
COSTUME
BOOK

40 Complete Patterns to Amaze & Amuse

■■■■■

Michelle Lipson & Friends

A Sterling/Lark Book
Sterling Publishing Co., Inc.   New York

TABLE OF CONTENTS

INTRODUCTION 6

THE BASICS
    Fabrics and Accessories.....................7
    Sizing 7
    Enlarging Patterns 7
    Cutting 8
    Bias Tape.....................................8
    Hot Glue Gun 9
    Painting Fabric 9
    Safety 9

IN DAYS OF OLD
    Photo Gallery 10
    His Royal Majesty 17
    Lady in Waiting 18
    Robin Hood 21
    Maid Marian...............................23
    Dragonslayer 24
    Merlin the Magician 27
    Court Jester.................................29
    Pixie Prankster 33

BIRDS AND BEASTS
    Photo Gallery 36
    Bat Attitude................................43
    Beautiful Butterfly 43
    The Firebird................................45
    Happy Toad.................................48
    Jumbo Elephant 50
    Jungle Cat...................................52
    Gorilla in a Monkeysuit 55

MUNCHIE MADNESS

 Photo Gallery 58

 Junkfood Junkie 62

 Meals on Wheels 62

 Sour Grapes 62

 Gingerbread Man's Revenge 63

 The Refrigerator 64

THE DARK SIDE

 Photo Gallery 66

 Wicked Witch 73

 Weird Warlock 76

 The Mummy 78

 Muscle Maniac 80

 Dreaded Cockroach 81

 The Cyclops..86

 Bog Monster 90

 Chinese Dragon 92

OUT OF THIS WORLD

 Photo Gallery 94

 Self Portrait 105

 Planet Earth 106

 Lucky Lindy 108

 Little Angel 112

 Wishing Star..114

 Rock Star...116

 Space Cadet 118

 Two-Headed Alien 120

 Captain Gadget..122

 The Machine...123

 No. 2 Pencil 125

 Blast Off 126

BIBLIOGRAPHY..127

CREDITS...128

INDEX 128

Make believe is as important for children as eating vegetables. A costume can be a child's key to the world of make believe, unlocking the door to a place where one can play and dream, be creative and practice growing up. It's the place of adventure where children can be brave, strong and very wise, a place to try out different personalities, to be a king, an elephant, or a monster.

Even as adults we enjoy dressing up for Halloween, masquerade parties, or "carnival."

It's fun and free, and a delightful way to celebrate. Even people who are ordinarily reserved will begin to act in character once they put on a costume. Put a child in a costume, one they have always dreamed of—perhaps a horrible creature like a cyclops. Suddenly, that quiet, sweet, well-mannered child becomes a growling, jumping, ferocious monster. Beware, the fun could go on for hours.

As you look through this book, keep in mind that some costumes will be more suitable for particular children than others. For example, a very young child will be happier with a simple costume, which is easy to put on and take off. If this can be accomplished independently by the child, it is even better. As a child matures, they can manage more complicated outfits. In fact, they often demand that their costumes have more and more details.

While there is great variety in the occasions for wearing costumes—parties, plays, parades, Halloween—they are not just for special events. Many of the costumes in this book would be a fine addition to a dress-up box, which can be filled with cast-off clothing, hats and props. Open up the dress-up box on a rainy afternoon and enter the land of make believe. Even costumes that are sewn for special occasions can be put in the dress-up box and played with over and over again.

Comfortable, fun-to-wear costumes promote the enthusiastic liveliness of children. The joy of creating as well as wearing costumes lies most of all in the playful experimentation with ideas that are new and your own. Accuracy and finishing details don't matter near as much as inspiration. Ask your children what they want—they'll probably commission your best work.

Before starting a project, carefully read the instructions and assembly diagrams. Visualize each step. Do each step in the sequence noted. Note the materials needed and gather together all fabrics and notions before beginning the costume.

Do not be afraid to make substitutions. Many of the projects in this book can be constructed with alternative materials. Glue (hot glue, fabric glue, etc.) can often be used instead of stitching. Cardboard, plastics, crepe paper and felt can be substituted for woven fabrics. Remember that the weight and stiffness of a fabric can be important to the success of a project, so do not substitute a lightweight, soft fabric for a heavyweight stiff fabric.

Fabrics and Accessories

You will frequently find that costume fabric is a hidden treasure waiting to be discovered in some old clothing or unused sheets, curtains or tablecloths. Your special material may be waiting at a yard sale, thrift shop, or the discount table of your local fabric store. You may occasionally find unusual pieces that inspire some new costume you'd never even dreamed of.

As you are collecting materials to construct your costume, be on the lookout for accessories: colorful socks and tights, feathers, jewelry, shoes, hats, and belts. Start saving things that you might ordinarily throw

away: plastic containers, old sponges, egg cartons, cardboard, beads, buttons, buckles, ribbons and cork. View each cast-off with a fresh eye for new uses. Although many of the costumes in this book do not start with cast-off clothing, many times you can substitute clothing for a lot of new construction.

Sizing

The scope of this book does not allow patterns for every size child. The patterns in this book are shown at various scales on graphs so that they can be enlarged to any size child. A 5 percent increase will enlarge a pattern to the next size.

An oversized costume is dangerous, and a closely fitted costume is uncomfortable. To determine the length of the costume, measure the child, then lengthen your pattern to correspond. A

shirt or a pair of pants should be lengthened at the hem. For the width of a garment, measure at the shoulders and hips, and enlarge the pattern accordingly.

Hats can be scaled directly by using the hat band size. Hat size is determined by measuring the head just above the eyebrows. It is better to make a hat a little too large rather than too small. If a hat is too large you can make it smaller by placing paper, cloth strips or foam rubber inside the band section. The foam rubber is excellent because it keeps the hat more firmly on the head.

Enlarging Patterns

You will need to draw full size patterns before you can begin construction of most of the costumes in this book. You are best advised to purchase a roll of inexpensive tracing paper on which to draw your patterns.

This paper is easy to pin to fabric, yet durable enough to use many times. However, you can use a heavy felt-tip marker on newspaper if you prefer.

The pattern pieces are printed on a graph so that you can transfer them to the size you need. Measure the corresponding points of the pattern on your child to determine the ratio for enlargement. For example, if your child is 12" from neckline to waistline and there are 6 squares of the graph on the pattern drawing between those points, then 1 square = 2 inches. Draw your own grid on large paper to the proper scale, then transfer the pattern lines proportionately from the small squares in the book to the larger squares on your full-size paper.

Although the pattern pieces are shown within a rectangular graph, this is not a fabric layout. The grain of the fabric is usually indicated by a double-pointed arrow. You will need to transfer all re-scaled pattern pieces onto the fabric and arrange them to fit.

Before you cut your fabric, pin your pattern together and fit them on the child to check for proper size. If alterations are needed, make them on the paper pattern at this time.

Cutting

Pattern pieces should be cut along solid lines and around notches. Review each pattern to determine how many pieces need to be cut from each pattern. Frequently pattern pieces will specify using the same piece for main fabric, lining, and interfacing. Foam pattern pieces are specified with a dotted line.

When cutting fabric on a fold, or two pieces from the same pattern, fold the fabric with selvages together and right sides facing. Lay your pattern on your fabric. Move the pieces around until you are satisfied that you will be able to cut all the pieces that you need. Using sharp shears or a rotary knife and mat, cut the fabric accurately following the solid line and around notches.

Many of the projects in this book use foam to provide support and structure to the costume. 1/2" (1.3 cm) upholstery foam is recommended for these projects because it is readily available, easily cut with scissors and light in weight. In general, the foam will be sandwiched between a lining and fabric, similar to a pillow in a pillow case. Follow these guidelines:

1. Cut out paper patterns for the foam pieces along the dotted lines.

2. Place each pattern on the foam sheet, moving the pieces around until you have a satisfactory layout.

3. Holding the pattern in place, trace the outline of the pattern on the foam with chalk or a felt tip marker.

4. Repeat the process until all foam pieces required for a costume have been cut.

5. Cut foam using sharp shears on inside of marked lines.

Important: Always check individual pattern instructions for seam allowance (the distance between cutting line and seam line). If no seam allowance is specified, use a standard 1/4" (6mm) margin for all seams.

Bias Tape

Applying bias tape is an excellent method for finishing edges of capes and necklines. It is sturdy and can withstand lots of wear. A word about technique should prove useful.

To prevent curved edges from stretching, stitch 1/4" (6 mm) from raw edges. Open out one folded edge of the bias tape. Pin bias tape to raw edge. Stitch 3/8" (1 cm) from edge. Trim and clip seam. Turn bias tape to inside along seams. Press and baste. Stitch close to basted edge.

GUIDE TO SYMBOLS

· · · · · · · · Cutting line foam

——— Cutting line

—△— Symbols to match
 o

—·—·—· Fold line

— — — — Machine quilt or stitching line

◄———► Grain line

Hot Glue Gun

A hot glue gun is quite a useful and versatile tool for costume construction. It is easy to use, inexpensive and very effective in joining fabric, cardboard, trim and other add-on elements. Costumes constructed of fabric and joined with hot glue can be washed without weakening the bond. Hot glue guns and glue can be purchased in craft and hobby shops, fabric stores and hardware stores.

Painting Fabric

Fabric paints are simply pigments suspended in a liquid binder. The binder is the means by which the pigment is held onto the fibers of the fabric. Here are some basic guidelines:

1. Pre-wash the fabric.
2. Transfer your design to the fabric using chalk, a water soluble fabric marker or a soft pencil.
3. Cover your work surface with newspaper or plastic garbage bags.
4. Test your paints on a scrap of fabric.
5. Apply the paint using a brush or squeeze bottle. When the painting is completed, allow the fabric to dry completely. To help set the paint, iron the reverse side of the fabric. Fabric paints that air-dry do not need to be heat set. Follow the manufacturer's directions.

Safety

Although some of the costumes in this book depart from strict safety practices, it's important to remember some common sense guidelines.

1. Make sure that the child can easily walk without tripping, entangling their feet or falling. Avoid costumes that drag on the floor, high heels or shoes that are oversized and poorly fitted.
2. Costumes should be lightweight and large enough so that warm clothing can be worn underneath if it's cold outside. Minimize fake fur and heavy fabric that can make a child hot and fussy.
3. Wigs, beards, masks and hats should be fastened securely, so that they don't obscure a child's vision.
4. If a costume is to be worn at night, sew reflective tape to the costume.
5. To make fabric fire resistant, dip it into a solution of 2.5L (2 quarts) warm water, 200ml (7 oz) borax and 85ml (3 oz) boric acid, then drip dry and iron. This must be reapplied each time a costume is washed.
6. To make paper or cardboard fire resistant, dip it into a solution of 2.5 L (2 quarts) warm water, 22 grams sulphate of ammonia, 84 grams boric acid crystals, 56 grams borax, then drip dry.
7. Facial makeup is preferable to masks for younger children. Non-toxic/hypoallergenic makeup is now widely available, especially at Halloween. You can make your own non-toxic makeup by mixing food coloring with one part soft shortening to two parts cornstarch.

IN DAYS OF OLD

HIS ROYAL MAJESTY

See instructions on page 17.

Old King Cole
Was a merry old soul,
And a merry old soul
was he.

> – Mother Goose

LADY IN WAITING

See instructions on page 18.

Fairy tales are filled with stories of princesses—frequently beset with problems to overcome, but always dressed in wonderful finery. Here is a costume for an elegant, witty and clever princess. Perhaps you know one.

ROBIN HOOD

See instructions on page 21.

This legend has made so many comebacks, there may be as many adults as children who'd like to don the forest green and take up archery.

MAID MARIAN

See instructions on page 23.

In olden days of chivalry and courtly love it was said, "The easy attainment of love makes it of little value." Dress up your little Maid Marian, and see if she plays hard to get.

DRAGONSLAYER

See instructions on page 24.

Saint George and the...serpent? Okay, worm. This splendid knight is obviously in training, and will face a bigger foe another day.

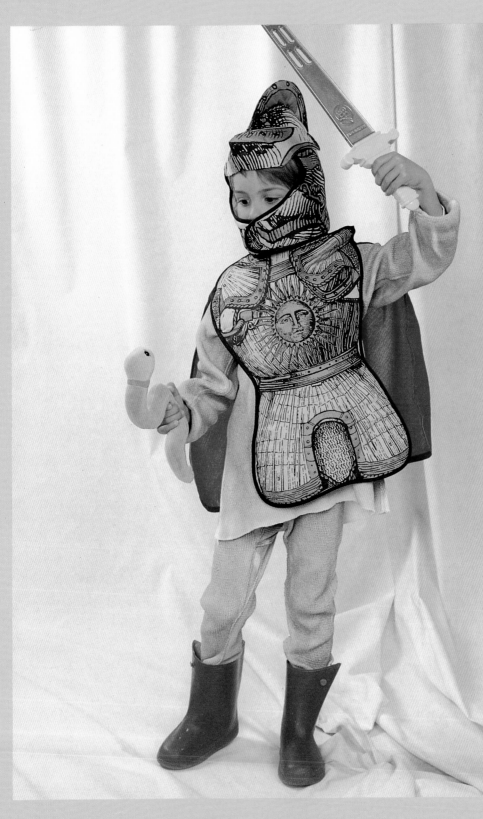

MERLIN THE MAGICIAN

See instructions on page 27.

King Arthur would be pleased to know how many young sorcerers' apprentices are striving to keep Merlin's tradition alive. And after all, who believes in magic more than a child?

COURT JESTER

See instructions on page 29.

It's hard to believe nowadays that a silly hat and checkered suit used to bring laughter and merriment to kings and their courtiers. Jesters added comic relief to the Dark Ages with spontaneous wit, funny faces and acrobatic antics.

PIXIE PRANKSTER

See instructions on page 33.

Pixies are fairies who were first mentioned in old stories told in England. They dance in the moonlight, blow out candles, tap on walls to frighten people, love water and lead people astray—especially at night.

HIS ROYAL MAJESTY

See Photo on page 10.

FABRIC

> 5/8 yd. (57.2 cm) Red velour
> 1/4 yd. (22.8 cm) Gold felt
> 1 yd (91.4 cm) Iron-on interfacing
> 1 1/2" x 24" (3.8 x 61 cm) White fake fur

NOTIONS

> 8 22.5 x 40 mm Diamond acrylic mirrors
> Small fake rubies
> 4 Long pipecleaners

ACCESSORIES

> Cape (see instructions for *Warlock*)
> Tunic (see instructions for *Cyclops*)
> Add fake fur trim to tunic with hot glue

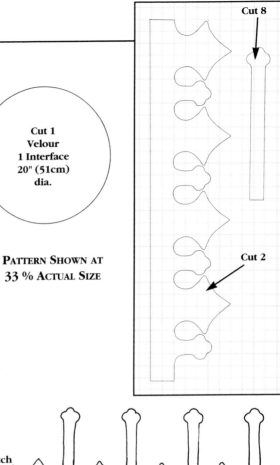

Cut 1
Velour
1 Interface
20" (51cm)
dia.

PATTERN SHOWN AT
33 % ACTUAL SIZE

1

❖ Apply iron-on interfacing to felt and velour fabric. Cut out pattern pieces.

Note: Because of the complicated shapes of the crown, applying the interfacing to the fabric prior to cutting will simplify construction of this project.

2

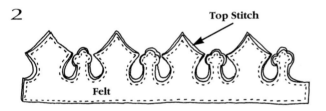

Top Stitch

Felt

❖ Right sides facing out, matching edges, pin felt crown pieces together. Topstitch 1/8" (3 mm) from edge.

3

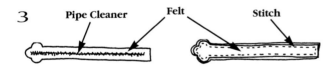

Pipe Cleaner   Felt   Stitch

❖ Cut pipecleaner to 9-1/2" (24.2 cm).

❖ Place pipecleaner on interfacing side of strip, 1/2" (1.3 cm) from bottom. Place another felt strip on top (right sides facing out).

❖ Topstitch 1/8" (3mm) from edge.

4

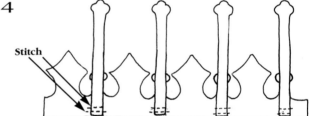

Stitch

❖ Place strips as shown, matching bottom of strip to bottom of crown. Stitch 1/4" (6 mm) from edge. Stitch 1/8" (3 mm) from edge.

5

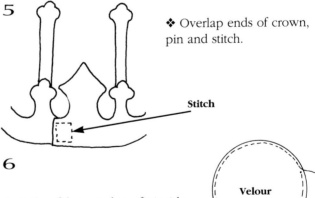

❖ Overlap ends of crown, pin and stitch.

Stitch

6

❖ Gather fabric circle to fit inside diameter of crown. Baste.

Velour

7

❖ Right sides facing out, place fabric circle inside of crown. Match gathered edge of fabric circle to bottom of crown. Stitch together 1/4" (6 mm) from edge.

❖ Glue 1 1/2" x 24" (3.8 x 61 cm) of white fake fur to bottom of crown.

❖ Glue top of strips together.

❖ Glue plastic jewels in place.

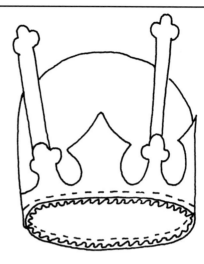

LADY IN WAITING

See Photo on page 11.

FABRIC

    2 yds. (1.8 m) Brocade or inexpensive imitation
    1-1/2 yd (1.4 m) Pink satin
    1 yd. of 1/8" (0.9 m of 3 mm) Pink satin ribbon
    32" x 24" (81 x 61 cm) Lightweight sheer fabric

NOTIONS

    1/2 yd. of 1/4" (46 cm of 6 mm) Elastic
    12 1/2" (1.3 cm) White plastic curtain rings

SEAM ALLOWANCE

    1/2" (1.3 cm)

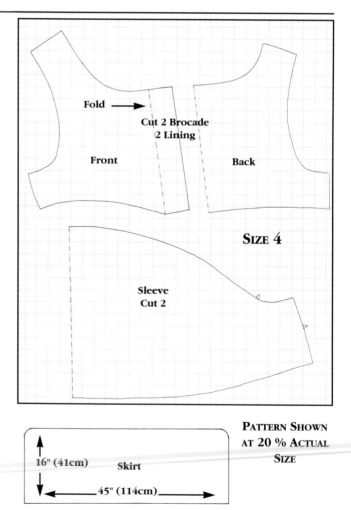

SIZE 4

PATTERN SHOWN AT 20 % ACTUAL SIZE

1

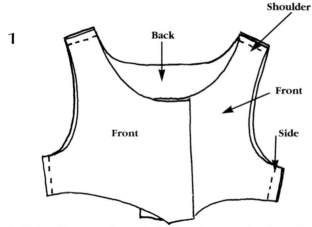

❖ Right sides together, pin bodice fronts to back of bodice. Stitch shoulder and side seams. Press seams open.

❖ Repeat for lining.

2

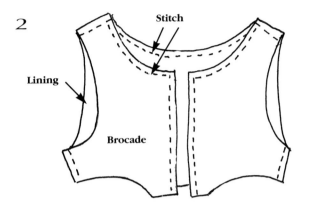

❖ Right sides together, matching seams, pin bodice assembly to lining. Stitch along front and neckline. Trim and clip seams. Turn right side out. Press.

❖ Baste remaining seams together.

3

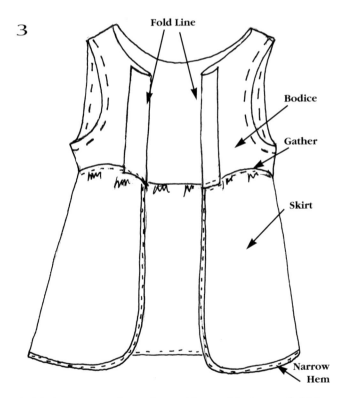

❖ Stitch a narrow hem along sides and bottom of skirt.

❖ Gather top of skirt. Right sides together, pin skirt to bodice. Match front of skirt to front fold line on bodice. Fold front bodice as shown. Stitch. Press.

4

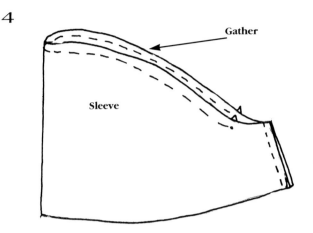

❖ Gather sleeves from notch to notch.

❖ Right sides together, pin and stitch sleeve seam. Turn up 1/2" casing on bottom of sleeve. Stitch close to edge to create casing for elastic. Leave opening to insert elastic. Size elastic to fit upper arm of child. Insert, and stitch ends of elastic together.

❖ Right sides together, match gathered sleeve edge to armhole in bodice. Pin and stitch.

❖ Repeat for remaining sleeve.

❖ Cut strips from pink satin 2-1/4" x 8" (5.7 x 20.3 cm). Fold strips in half lengthwise. Stitch, turn right sides out. Stitch to sleeve as shown in photograph.

❖ Stitch 6 rings to each side of front bodice. Lace 1/8" (3 mm) ribbon through rings to fasten.

❖ Construct hat as described in *Maid Marian* costume. Finish the edges of 36" x 24" (81 x 61 cm) sheer fabric. Pinch a point just off center and stitch (or glue) it to point of hat.

To make the underskirt, you will need:

FABRIC
1-1/2 yd. of 108" wide (1.4 m of 2.75 m) Tulle
NOTIONS
Leotard
Ball point needle (for stretchy fabric)
14 yds. of 5/8" (12.8 m of 1.6 cm) Satin ribbon

5

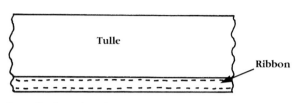

❖ Cut tulle into 4 strips:
        108" x 7" (17.8 cm)
        108" x 11-1/2" (29 cm)
        108" x 14-1/2" (37 cm)
        108" x 17-1/2" (44.5 cm)

❖ Edgestitch edges of ribbon to bottom edge of each tulle strip.

6

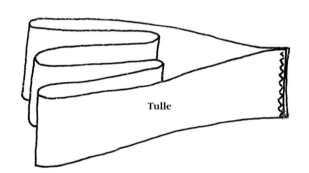

❖ Right sides together, using a small zigzag stitch, stitch short edges of each tulle strip together.

❖ Find waist of leotard by tying a string around the waist of the child while they are wearing it. Mark with a watersoluble marker or chalk.

7

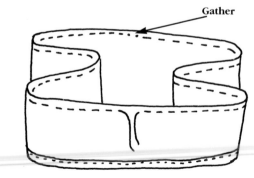

❖ Gather long edge of 7" (17.8 cm) wide tulle strip. Repeat for remaining strips.

8

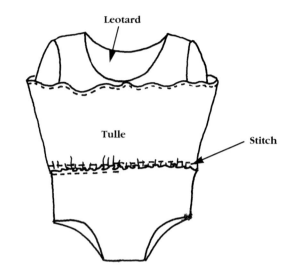

❖ Right sides together, pin and baste gathered strip evenly around waist of leotard. Repeat for remaining strips. Attach strips from smallest to largest. Use a zigzag stitch over basting through all layers of tulle and leotard.

9

❖ Stitch 24" (61 cm) ribbon to each shoulder at the neckline. Tie the ribbon onto a bow.

See Photo on page 12.

FABRIC

    2 yds. (1.8 m) Green poly/cotton
    1/2 yd. (46 cm) Heavyweight iron-on
        interfacing
    4 yds. (3.7 m) Red double-fold bias tape
    1/2 yd. (46 cm) Iron-on interfacing (collar)
    4" x 11" (10 x 28 cm) Fusible web
    8" x 11" (20 x 28 cm) Red poly/cotton

NOTIONS

    12" (30.5 cm) Pipecleaner

Pattern diagrams for Robin Hood & Maid Marian

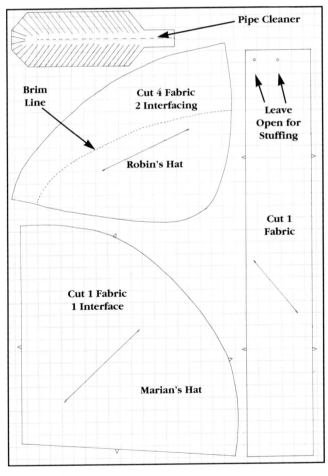

Brim Line

Cut 4 Fabric 2 Interfacing

Leave Open for Stuffing

Pipe Cleaner

Robin's Hat

Cut 1 Fabric

Cut 1 Fabric 1 Interface

Marian's Hat

PATTERN SHOWN AT
15 % ACTUAL SIZE

See *Pixie* for collar instructions, but rather than applying bias tape to the neckline, attach it to the cape as described in cape instructions for the *Warlock*.

To construct the cape, apply bias tape to sides and bottom of *Wizard* cape.

Here's how to make the hat.

1

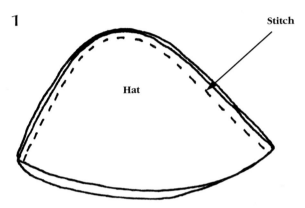

Stitch

Hat

❖ Apply iron-on interfacing to two matching hat pieces.

❖ Right sides together, pin and stitch matching halves of hat. Trim and clip seams. Turn and press.

❖ Repeat for lining.

2

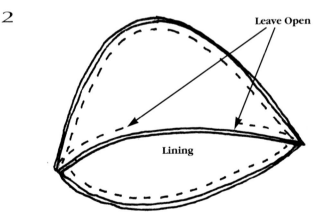

Leave Open

Lining

❖ Right sides together, match raw edge of lining to raw edge of hat. Pin and stitch. Leave opening for turning.

❖ Turn hat to right side through opening.

❖ Turn seam allowance at opening to inside. Press. Baste.

❖ Edgestitch bottom edge of hat.

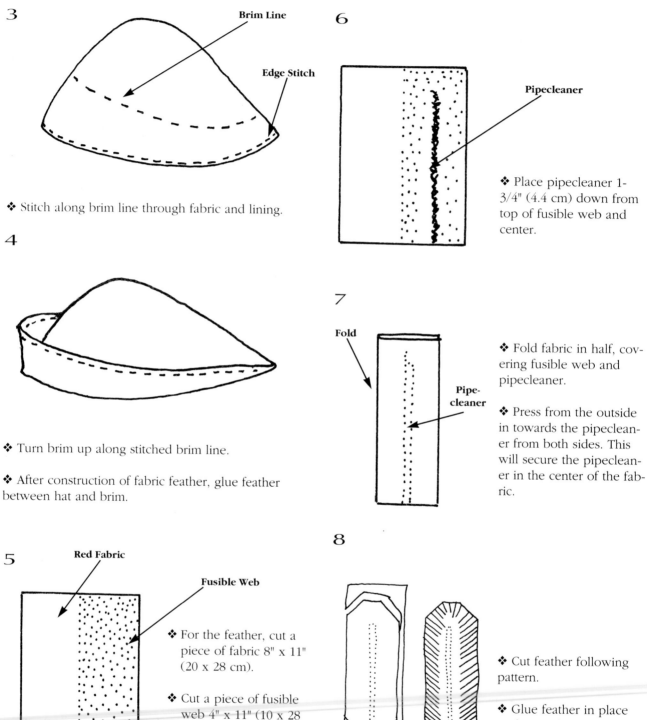

3

Brim Line

Edge Stitch

❖ Stitch along brim line through fabric and lining.

4

❖ Turn brim up along stitched brim line.

❖ After construction of fabric feather, glue feather between hat and brim.

5

Red Fabric

Fusible Web

❖ For the feather, cut a piece of fabric 8" x 11" (20 x 28 cm).

❖ Cut a piece of fusible web 4" x 11" (10 x 28 cm).

6

Pipecleaner

❖ Place pipecleaner 1-3/4" (4.4 cm) down from top of fusible web and center.

7

Fold

Pipe-cleaner

❖ Fold fabric in half, covering fusible web and pipecleaner.

❖ Press from the outside in towards the pipecleaner from both sides. This will secure the pipecleaner in the center of the fabric.

8

❖ Cut feather following pattern.

❖ Glue feather in place on hat as shown in photo.

See Photo on page 12, pattern on page 21.

FABRIC

14" x 14" (35 x 35 cm) Pink poly/cotton
14" x 14" (35 x 35 cm) Heavyweight iron-on
 interfacing
4" x 28" (10 x 71 cm) Silver lamé
1 oz. Polyester fiberfill stuffing

NOTIONS

1 yd. of 1/8" (91 cm of 3 mm) Pink ribbon
3 Large sequin bangles

SEAM ALLOWANCE

1/2" (1.3 cm)

1

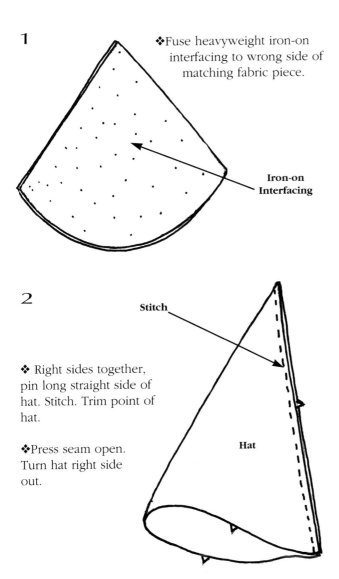

❖Fuse heavyweight iron-on
 interfacing to wrong side of
 matching fabric piece.

Iron-on Interfacing

2

Stitch

❖ Right sides together,
pin long straight side of
hat. Stitch. Trim point of
hat.

❖Press seam open.
Turn hat right side
out.

Hat

3

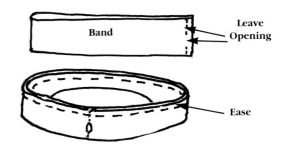

Band

Leave Opening

Ease

❖ Right sides together, fold band in half as shown.
Stitch. Leave opening between circles as shown. Press
seam open.

❖ Fold band, wrong sides together. Pin and easestitch
raw edges of band.

4

❖ Pin hat band to right side of hat,
matching seams, and notches.
Adjust ease on band as needed.
Stitch. Trim seam. Zigzag raw
edge of seam. Press seam
toward hat.

❖ Stuff hat band with
small amounts of fiber-
fill. Stitch opening in
band closed.

Stitch

Hat

Band

5

❖ Cut 3 different lengths of the yard (.9 m) of ribbon.
Hand stitch ribbons to point of hat. Tie bangles to end.

❖ If hat won't stand up, hot glue a thin small wooden
dowel inside the cone.

DRAGONSLAYER

See Photo on page 13.

FABRIC

1 yd. (91 cm) Quilted fabric
1 yd. (91 cm) Grey poly/cotton
3/4 yd. (69 cm) Red poly/cotton

NOTIONS

2-1/2 yds. (2.3 m) Purple bias tape
2 sets of 1/2" (1.3 cm) Hook and loop tape
Fabric paints or markers (black, gold)

ACCESSORIES

Rib-knit long johns, spray painted silver
Boots and sword

First, cut out pieces of grey fabric that need to be painted. Apply paint, following the designs on the pattern.

2

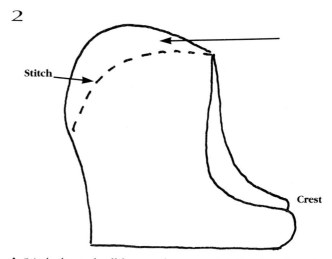

❖ Stitch through all layers along crest, following dotted line as shown.

1

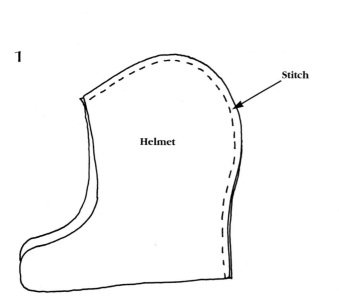

❖ Right sides together, pin and stitch helmet halves together. Clip and trim seam. Turn right side out. Press.

❖ Repeat for quilted lining. Do not turn.

❖ Right sides facing, matching seams, pin quilted lining to fabric.

❖ Stitch helmet to lining. Leave opening between double notches. Trim seams. Turn right side out through opening. Turn seam allowance to inside at opening. Baste opening closed. Top stitch edge of helmet.

3

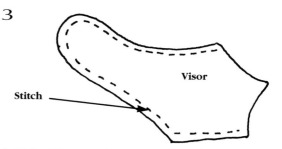

❖ Right sides together, pin and stitch visor to lining. Trim seams and turn right sides out.

❖ Repeat for remaining half of visor.

4

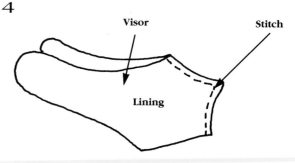

❖ Right sides together, stitch visor halves together. Turn right side out. Press. Edgestitch seam.

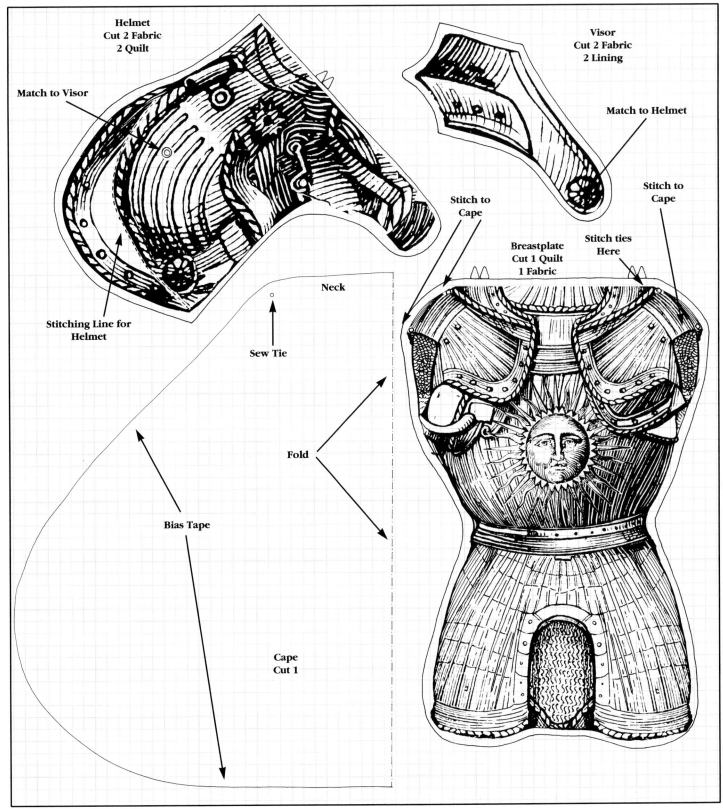

Helmet
Cut 2 Fabric
2 Quilt

Match to Visor

Visor
Cut 2 Fabric
2 Lining

Match to Helmet

Stitching Line for Helmet

Stitch to Cape

Stitch to Cape

Stitch ties Here

Breastplate
Cut 1 Quilt
1 Fabric

Neck

Sew Tie

Fold

Bias Tape

Cape
Cut 1

PATTERN SHOWN AT
26 % ACTUAL SIZE

5

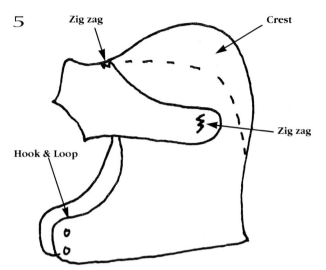

❖ Matching circles, pin visor to helmet. Stitch (zigzag) at circle and at center front to secure visor to helmet.

❖ Glue hook and loop dots to helmet to fasten.

6

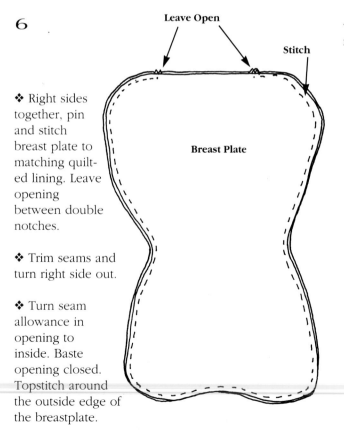

❖ Right sides together, pin and stitch breast plate to matching quilted lining. Leave opening between double notches.

❖ Trim seams and turn right side out.

❖ Turn seam allowance in opening to inside. Baste opening closed. Topstitch around the outside edge of the breastplate.

7

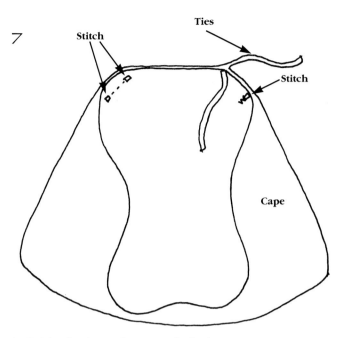

❖ Finish all edges of cape with the bias tape.

❖ Stitch breastplate to cape as shown. Stitch ties at neck.

See Photo on page 14.

FABRIC

1-1/2 yd. of 60" (1.4 m of 152 cm) Purple
  velour
5/8 yd. (57.2 cm) White fake fur
3/4 yd. (69 cm) Lining
Scraps of silver lamé

NOTIONS

18" x 18" (45.7 x 45.7 cm) Fusible web
1 yd. (91.4 cm) Single-fold bias tape (purple)
1/2 yd. of 3/8" (46 cm of 1 cm) Elastic
3 oz. Polyester fiberfill batting

For hat, see instructions for *Maid Marian*. Cut the hat band from fake fur.

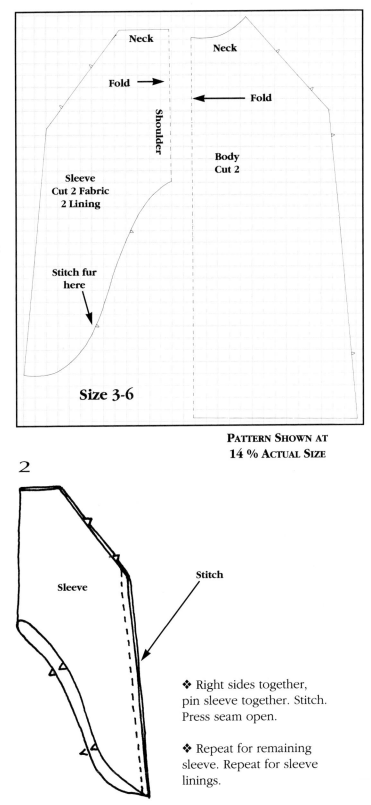

**PATTERN SHOWN AT
14 % ACTUAL SIZE**

1

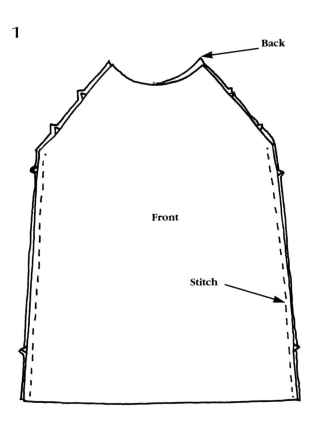

❖ Right sides together, pin front to back at side seams. Stitch. Press seams open.

2

❖ Right sides together, pin sleeve together. Stitch. Press seam open.

❖ Repeat for remaining sleeve. Repeat for sleeve linings.

3

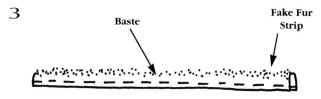

❖ Fold 2-1/2" x 45" (6.4 x 114 cm) strip in half, right sides facing out. Baste 1/4" (6 mm) from raw edge. Cut strip in 2 pieces 22-1/2" (57.2 cm).

4

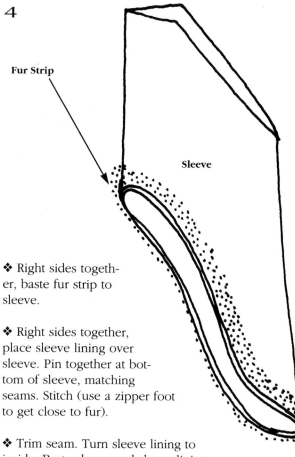

❖ Right sides together, baste fur strip to sleeve.

❖ Right sides together, place sleeve lining over sleeve. Pin together at bottom of sleeve, matching seams. Stitch (use a zipper foot to get close to fur).

❖ Trim seam. Turn sleeve lining to inside. Baste sleeve and sleeve lining together along raw edge.

❖ Repeat for remaining sleeve.

5

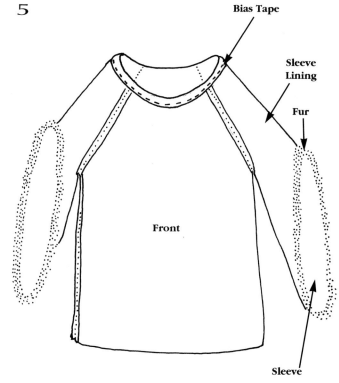

❖ Right sides together, pin sleeve assembly to front and back, match notches, stitch.

❖ Repeat for remaining sleeve.

❖ Right sides together, stitch bias tape to neck.

❖ Turn bias tape to inside, stitch close to folded edge. Leave an opening to insert elastic.

❖ Insert elastic into casing. Size to fit child's neck. Stitch ends of elastic together.

❖ Stitch casing closed.

❖ Cut out shapes from silver lamé which has been bonded to fusible web. Iron in place. *Note:* Use pressing cloth to protect metallic fabric.

See Photo on page 15.

FABRIC

13" x 9" (33 x 22.9 cm) Yellow felt
14" x 22" (35.6 x 55.9 cm) Red felt
14" x 22" (35.6 x 55.9 cm) Blue felt
14" x 6" (35.6 x 15.2 cm) Green felt

NOTIONS

2 Jingle bells
8" x 3/8" (20.3 x 1 cm) Ribbon
24" x 3/8" (61 x 1 cm) Elastic

SEAM ALLOWANCE

3/8" (1 cm)

1

❖ Right sides together, pin a yellow and a red hat piece together. Stitch. Repeat for remaining red and yellow pieces.

2

❖ Right sides together, match seams and pin yellow next to red. Stitch.

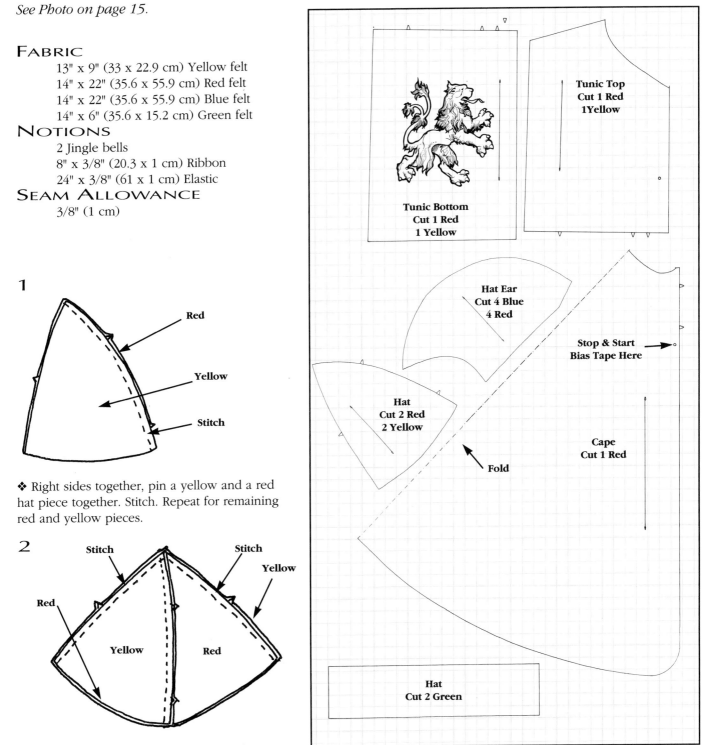

**PATTERN SHOWN AT
18 % ACTUAL SIZE**

3

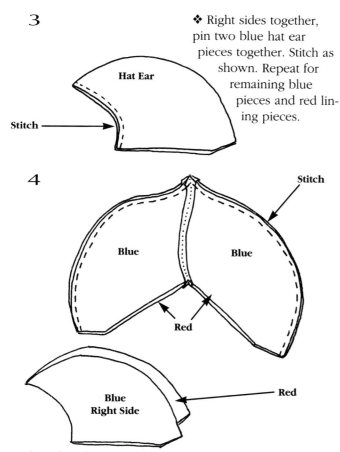

❖ Right sides together, pin two blue hat ear pieces together. Stitch as shown. Repeat for remaining blue pieces and red lining pieces.

4

❖ Right sides together, pin blue hat ear piece to red lining. Stitch. Clip seams and turn right side out. Press. (Red will be the inside lining.) Repeat for remaining pieces.

5

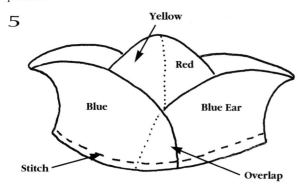

❖ Matching side seams, pin ear pieces to hat. Overlap ears in center. Stitch together along base of hat.

❖ Stitch through all thicknesses to secure ears to hat as shown.

6

❖ Right sides together, pin and stitch green hat band pieces together.

7

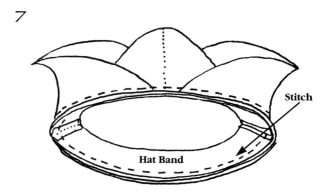

❖ Place hat band inside of hat, right side of band facing wrong side of hat. Pin and stitch.

8

❖ Overlap ends of elastic 1/2" (1.3 cm). Stitch together. Place elastic between hat band and body of hat. Stretch and pin to body of hat. Use a large zigzag stitch to stitch elastic to hat body. Do not stitch to green band.

9

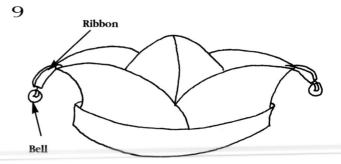

❖ Cut two pieces of ribbon 4" (10.2 cm) long. Thread bells through ribbons. Fold ribbons in half. Hot glue (or stitch) ribbons together and then to points on ears.

For the jester's tunic, you will need:

FABRIC
1-1/4 yd (111.8 cm) Red poly/cotton fabric
1/4 yd. (20.3 cm) Yellow poly/cotton fabric
4-1/2 yds. (4.1 m) Bias tape (double-fold)
5/8 yd. (57.2 cm) Purple felt

NOTIONS
Gold and black fabric paint or markers

12

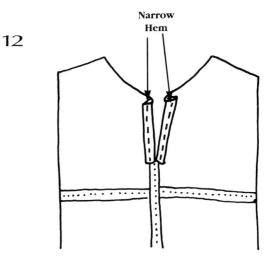

10

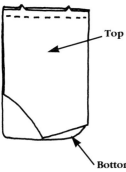

❖ To begin the tunic, place right sides together, matching notches of red front bottom to yellow front top, pin. Stitch. Press seam open.

❖ Repeat for yellow bottom and red top.

❖ Clip at circle.

❖ Narrow hem front opening.

13

11

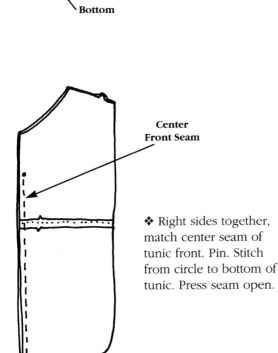

❖ Right sides together, match center seam of tunic front. Pin. Stitch from circle to bottom of tunic. Press seam open.

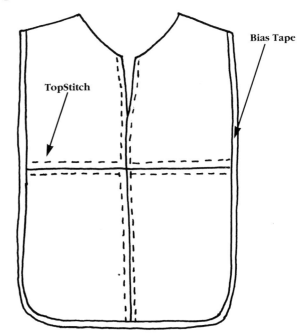

❖ Topstitch front of tunic, as shown.

❖ Apply bias tape binding to outside edges of tunic front.

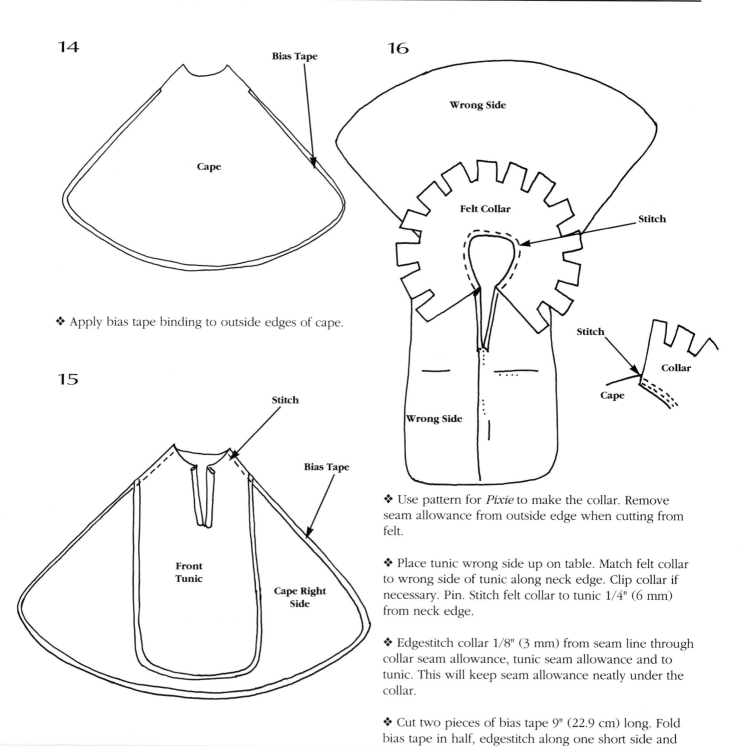

14

Bias Tape

Cape

❖ Apply bias tape binding to outside edges of cape.

15

Stitch

Bias Tape

Front
Tunic

Cape Right
Side

❖ Right sides together, pin tunic shoulder seams to cape. Pin. Stitch. Press.

16

Wrong Side

Felt Collar

Stitch

Wrong Side

Stitch

Collar

Cape

❖ Use pattern for *Pixie* to make the collar. Remove seam allowance from outside edge when cutting from felt.

❖ Place tunic wrong side up on table. Match felt collar to wrong side of tunic along neck edge. Clip collar if necessary. Pin. Stitch felt collar to tunic 1/4" (6 mm) from neck edge.

❖ Edgestitch collar 1/8" (3 mm) from seam line through collar seam allowance, tunic seam allowance and to tunic. This will keep seam allowance neatly under the collar.

❖ Cut two pieces of bias tape 9" (22.9 cm) long. Fold bias tape in half, edgestitch along one short side and the long side.

❖ Sew ties in place on front of tunic.

PIXIE PRANKSTER

See Photo on page 16.

FABRIC

24" x 15" (61 x 38.1 cm) Green poly/cotton
10" x 8" (25.4 x 20.3 cm) Pink poly/cotton
10" x 8" (25.4 x 20.3 cm) Polyester fiberfill batting
24" x 15" (61 x 38.1 cm) Iron-on interfacing
24" x 15" (61 x 38.1 cm) Felt

NOTIONS

1" (2.5 cm) dia. Jingle bell

ACCESSORIES

Green leotard & tights or sweatsuit

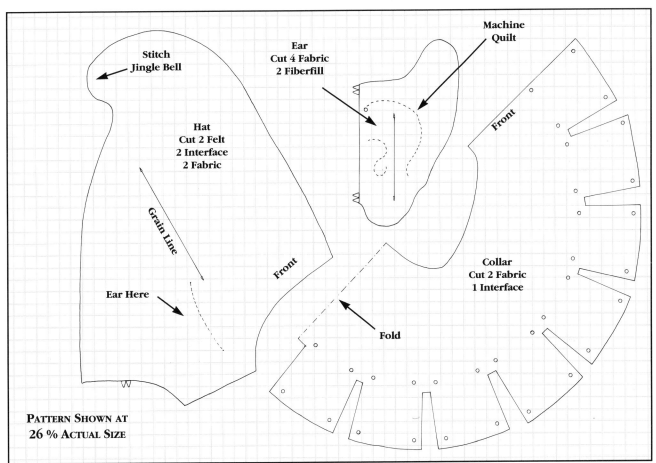

Stitch Jingle Bell

Ear
Cut 4 Fabric
2 Fiberfill

Machine Quilt

Front

Hat
Cut 2 Felt
2 Interface
2 Fabric

Grain Line

Front

Ear Here

Collar
Cut 2 Fabric
1 Interface

Fold

PATTERN SHOWN AT 26 % ACTUAL SIZE

1

❖ Right sides together, pin two ear pieces together, match fabric ears to polyester fiberfill batting ear. Stitch sandwich together, leave opening between double notches.

2

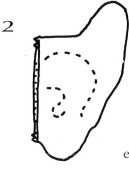

❖ Trim and clip seams. Turn ear right side out between fabric pieces. Press. Baste opening closed.

❖ Machine quilt ear as shown with dotted lines.

❖ Repeat above for remaining ear pieces.

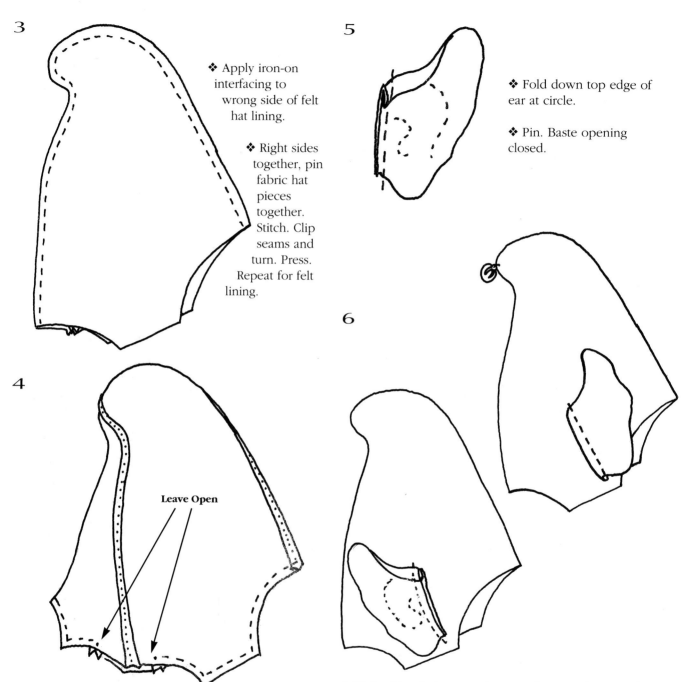

3

❖ Apply iron-on interfacing to wrong side of felt hat lining.

❖ Right sides together, pin fabric hat pieces together. Stitch. Clip seams and turn. Press. Repeat for felt lining.

4

Leave Open

5

❖ Fold down top edge of ear at circle.

❖ Pin. Baste opening closed.

6

❖ Right sides together, place felt hat lining inside hat. Match seams and pin raw edges together. Stitch, leaving opening between double notches. Trim and clip seam. Turn. Turn seam allowance at opening to inside. Hand stitch opening closed. Press.

❖ Right sides facing up, pin ear to hat, matching stitching line on ear to marked line on hat. Stitch. Trim seam. Press ear over raw edge on ear. Stitch 1/4" (6 mm) from previous stitching line. Repeat for remaining ear.

❖ Hand stitch jingle bell to point on hat.

For the Pixie Prankster's collar, you will need:

FABRIC

   5/8 yd.of 45" (57.2 of 114.3 cm) Green
      poly/cotton
   20" x 21" (50.8 x 53.3 cm) Iron-on
      interfacing

NOTIONS

   1 yd. (91.4 cm) Double-fold bias tape

8

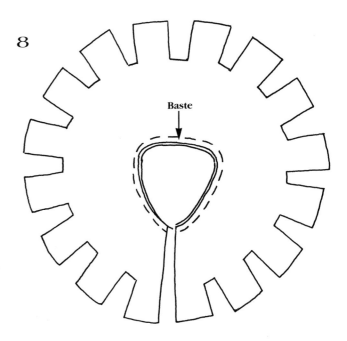

❖ Pin and baste raw edge of neckline together.

7

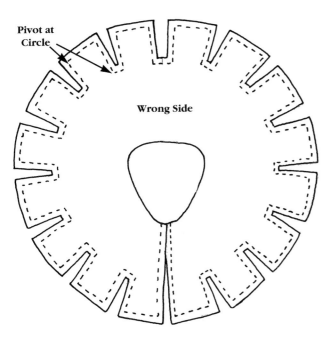

❖ First, apply iron-on interfacing to the under collar piece.

❖ Right sides together, pin collar pieces together. Stitch as shown, pivot needle at circles. Clip and trim seams.

❖ Turn collar right side out. Press.

9

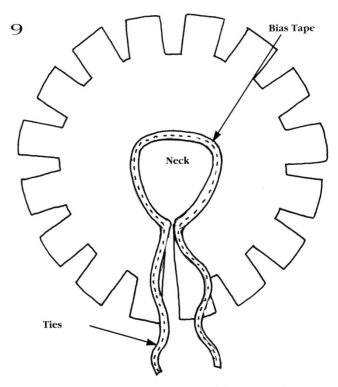

❖ Apply double-fold bias tape to neckline. Extend tape 8" (20.3 cm) at both ends of collar to use for ties.

BIRDS AND BEASTS

BAT ATTITUDE

See instructions on page 43.

Bats are creepy, scary, hang upside down in caves, and fly at night by radar. They are emulated by super-heroes, and envied by certain children possessed of... "the attitude."

BEAUTIFUL BUTTERFLY

See instructions on page 43.

Millions of Monarch butterflies migrate across the country annually. There is a town in California that has so many Monarch butterflies, they have a parade in their honor every year.

THE FIREBIRD

See instructions on page 45.

The legendary Phoenix is a magical bird that sets itself on fire, then rises from its own ashes even more beautiful than before. (Please see recipe for flame retardancy on page 9.)

HAPPY TOAD

See instructions on page 48.

Hoppity, hoppity, rib-bit, slurp, kerplop! Will somebody please kiss this frog and turn it back into a child before it has too much fun?

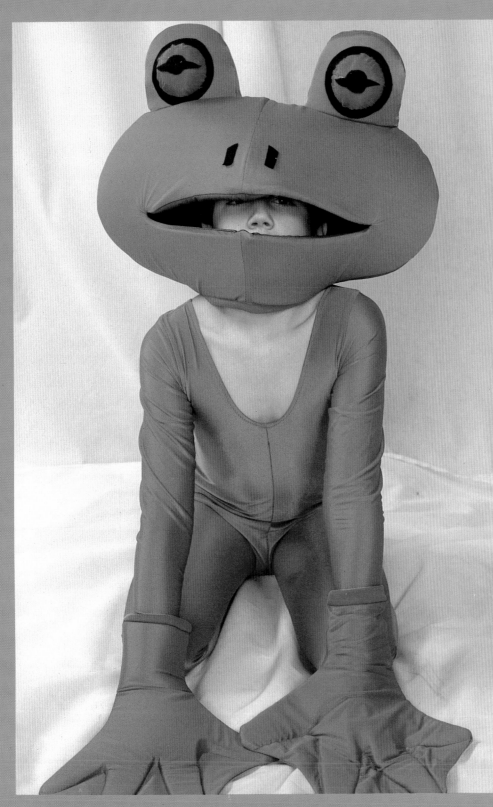

JUMBO ELEPHANT

See instructions on page 50.

For the child who just can't wait to grow up, here's an enormous opportunity. Elephants are the largest of land animals and can weigh up to 20,000 pounds!

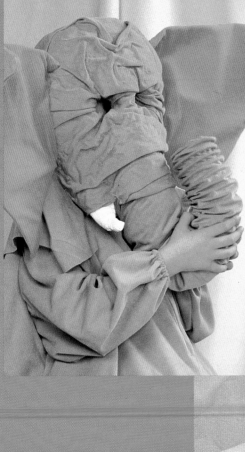

JUNGLE CAT

See instructions on page 52.

There was a young lady
   from Niger
Who smiled as she rode
   on a tiger,
They returned from the
   ride
With the lady inside
And the smile on the
   face of the tiger.

GORILLA IN A MONKEYSUIT

See instructions on page 55.

This uptown ape won't have to hang off the top of a skyscraper to get attention. But cousin Hairy the Gorilla will exude sophistication as he climbs one more rung on the evolutionary ladder.

Bat Attitude & Beautiful Butterfly

See Photos on pages 36 and 37.

For the *Bat* costume:

FABRIC

36" x 20" (91.4 x 50.8 cm) Black felt

1-1/2 yds. of 45" (137 of 114 cm) Light purple
poly/cotton fabric

NOTIONS

2" (5.1 cm) Red pom-poms

2 sets of 1/2" (1.3 cm) hook and loop dots

Black fabric paint or markers

1/2 yd. of 1/2" (46 of 1.3 cm) Black twill
tape

SEAM ALLOWANCE

1/2" (1.3 cm)

For the *Beautiful Butterfly*:

FABRIC

Scraps of purple and green felt, otherwise same
as *Bat*, except substitute: Red felt, Orange
poly/cotton, and purple pom-poms.

NOTIONS & SEAM ALLOWANCE

Same as Bat

1

❖ The bat is assembled in the same manner as the butterfly, except for the helmet.

❖ Before beginning construction, transfer wing design
to fabric.

❖ Use paint (or fabric markers) to apply design to bat
wings.

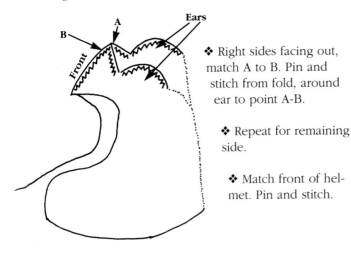

❖ Right sides facing out,
match A to B. Pin and
stitch from fold, around
ear to point A-B.

❖ Repeat for remaining
side.

❖ Match front of hel-
met. Pin and stitch.

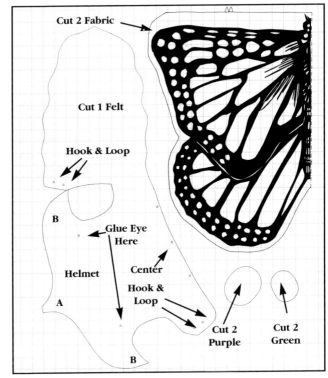

Pattern for Bat Attitude

Pattern for Beautiful Butterfly

2

❖ Apply image of butterfly to orange poly/cotton using black fabric paint or marker.

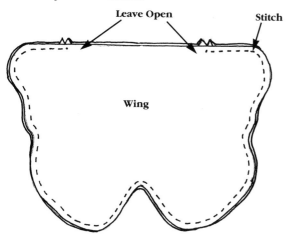

❖ Right sides together, pin and stitch wings together. Leave opening between double notches.

❖ Trim seams and turn right side out through opening.

❖ Turn seam allowance in opening to inside. Press entire wing.

❖ Baste opening closed.

3

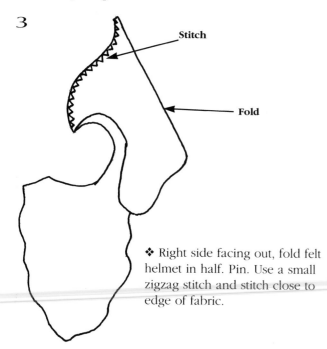

❖ Right side facing out, fold felt helmet in half. Pin. Use a small zigzag stitch and stitch close to edge of fabric.

4

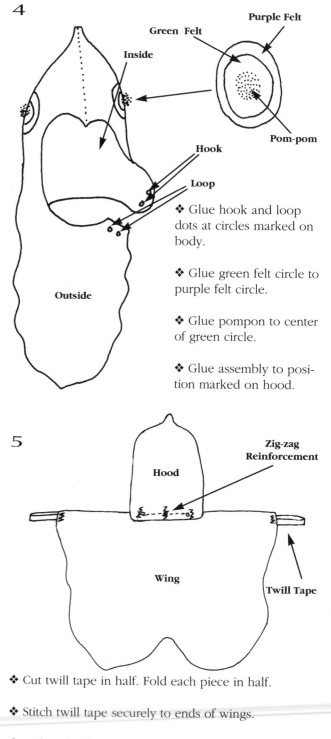

❖ Glue hook and loop dots at circles marked on body.

❖ Glue green felt circle to purple felt circle.

❖ Glue pompon to center of green circle.

❖ Glue assembly to position marked on hood.

5

❖ Cut twill tape in half. Fold each piece in half.

❖ Stitch twill tape securely to ends of wings.

❖ Right sides facing out, match center back of helmet and center back of wing. Reinforce using a zigzag stitch as shown.

THE FIREBIRD

See Photo on page 38.

FABRIC

> 2-1/2 yds. (2.3 m) Red satin
> 2-1/2 yds. (2.3 m) Yellow poly/cotton
> 2 yds. (1.8 m) Fusible web
> 2" x 4" (5 x 10 cm) Black felt

NOTIONS

> 1/2" (1.3 cm) Hook and loop dot
> 1 yd. (.9 m) Red bias tape
> 18" of 1/2" (46 of 1.3 cm) Black twill tape
> Hot glue and gun

It is easier to cut many of the pieces for this costume after they have been fused to their backing. Some pieces are fused to iron-on interfacing. Other pieces are bonded together with fusible web. Because of the complex shapes of these pieces, the following procedure for cutting is recommended.

For chest pieces A, B, C and beak pieces:
1. Trace pattern pieces on yellow fabric.
2. Lay piece of yellow fabric (uncut) on top of the sheet of iron-on interfacing.
3. Fuse pieces together.
4. Cut pieces following solid lines and around notches.

For helmet pieces B, C, D, E:
1. Trace pattern pieces on yellow fabric.
2. Lay piece of yellow fabric (uncut) on top of the sheet of fusible web.
3. Lay the fusible web on top of red fabric.
4. Fuse all pieces together.
5. Cut pieces following solid lines and around notches.

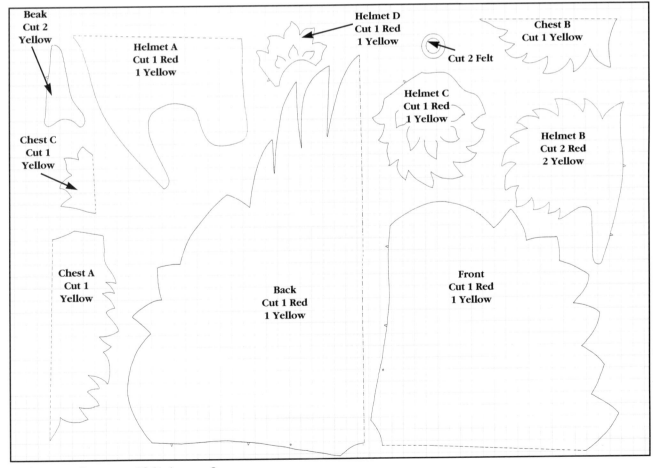

PATTERNS SHOWN AT 12 % ACTUAL SIZE

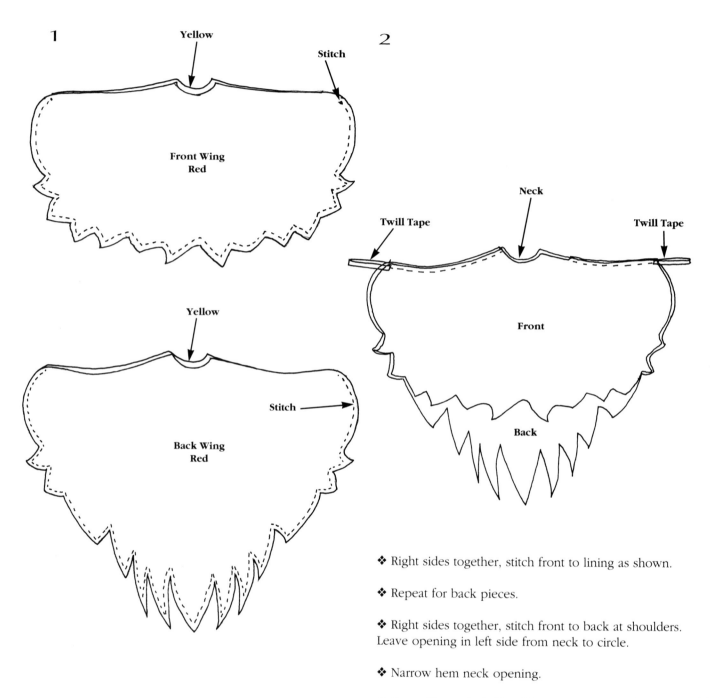

1

Yellow

Stitch

Front Wing
Red

Yellow

Stitch

Back Wing
Red

2

Neck

Twill Tape

Twill Tape

Front

Back

❖ Right sides together, stitch front to lining as shown.

❖ Repeat for back pieces.

❖ Right sides together, stitch front to back at shoulders. Leave opening in left side from neck to circle.

❖ Narrow hem neck opening.

❖ Cut twill tape in half. Fold each piece in half and stitch to wing tips.

❖ Right sides together, pin and stitch front wing to lining. Trim and clip seams. Turn right side out, and press.

❖ Repeat for back wing.

3

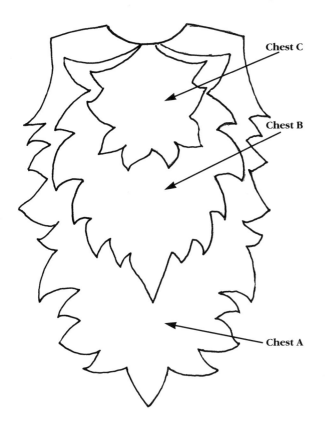

Chest C

Chest B

Chest A

❖ Layer chest pieces A, B, C as shown. Use fusible web strips to glue pieces together along center fold line.

❖ Baste chest pieces at neck edge, matching centers. Glue to front wing using fusible web strips.

❖ Apply bias tape to neck.

❖ Glue hook & loop dot at neck.

4

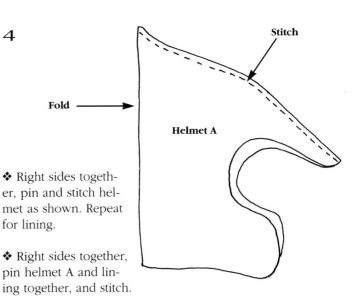

Stitch

Fold

Helmet A

❖ Right sides together, pin and stitch helmet as shown. Repeat for lining.

❖ Right sides together, pin helmet A and lining together, and stitch. Leave an opening for turning on lower back of helmet.

❖ Trim seams and turn. Press.

5

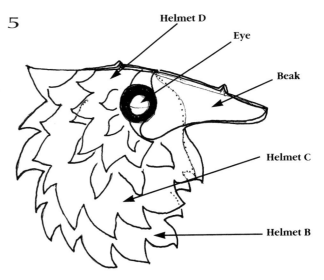

Helmet D

Eye

Beak

Helmet C

Helmet B

❖ Right sides together, matching notches, pin and stitch the remaining helmet pieces and beak.

❖ Following diagram, layer helmet pieces onto main helmet. Use hot glue to secure.

❖ Attach beak with hot glue.

❖ Attach felt eye with glue.

See Photo on page 39.

FABRIC

1-1/2 yd. (1.4 m) Green lycra or spandex
6" x 12" (15 cm x 30 cm) Red satin scrap
1/4 yd. (23 cm) Red knit ribbing
6" x 6" (15 x 15 cm) Black felt

NOTIONS

3" (7.6 cm) Plastic ball
1 yd. of 1/2" (91 of 1.3 cm) Foam rubber

ACCESSORIES

Swim flippers

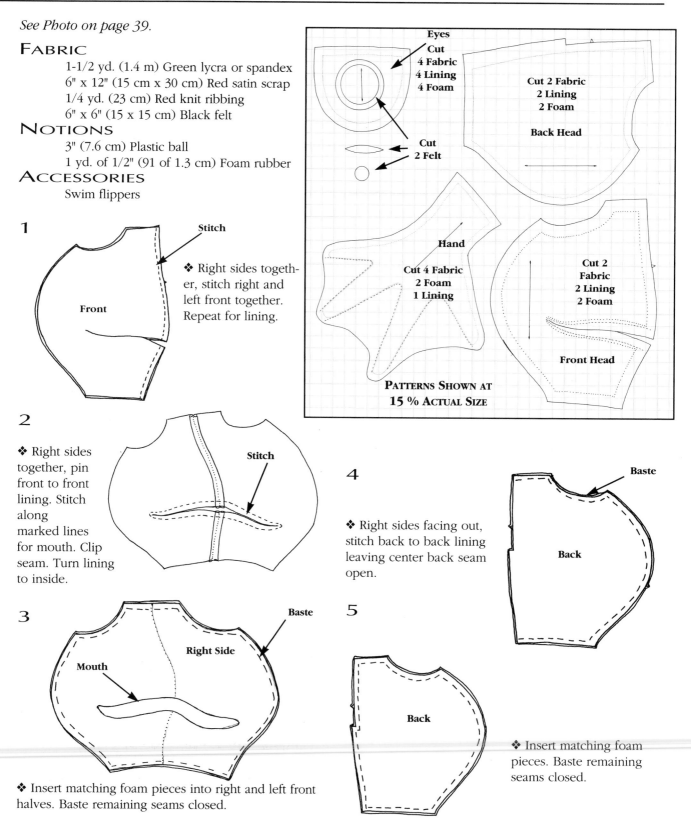

Eyes
Cut
4 Fabric
4 Lining
4 Foam

Cut 2 Fabric
2 Lining
2 Foam

Back Head

Cut
2 Felt

Hand
Cut 4 Fabric
2 Foam
1 Lining

Cut 2
Fabric
2 Lining
2 Foam

Front Head

PATTERNS SHOWN AT 15 % ACTUAL SIZE

1

Stitch

Front

❖ Right sides together, stitch right and left front together. Repeat for lining.

2

Stitch

❖ Right sides together, pin front to front lining. Stitch along marked lines for mouth. Clip seam. Turn lining to inside.

3

Baste

Right Side

Mouth

❖ Insert matching foam pieces into right and left front halves. Baste remaining seams closed.

4

Baste

Back

❖ Right sides facing out, stitch back to back lining leaving center back seam open.

5

Back

❖ Insert matching foam pieces. Baste remaining seams closed.

6

❖ Right sides together, stitch right and left back halves together, stopping at circle.

❖ Apply hook and loop tape to the back opening.

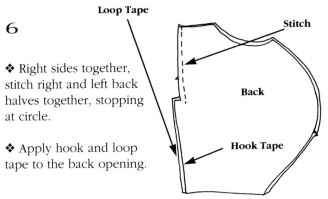

7

❖ Wrong sides together, stitch eyes together leaving opening along straight edge.

❖ Insert matching foam piece. Baste open seam closed.

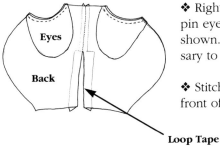

❖ Right sides together, pin eyes to back as shown. Clip where necessary to aid fit.

❖ Stitch. Repeat eyes on front of head.

8

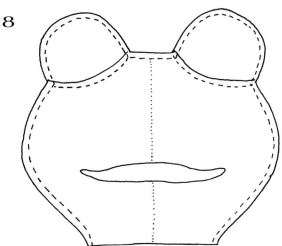

❖ Right sides together, stitch front to back at side, eye and upper edges. Trim seams, turn head right side out.

9

❖ For the neckband, cut a rectangle 17-1/2" x 6" (45 x 15 cm) from red rib knit.

❖ Fold neck band in half lengthwise, stitch ends in 1/4" (6 mm) seam. Fold band to measure 3" x 17" (7.6 x 43 cm), wrong sides facing. Baste raw edges together. Pin neck band to lower edge of frog's head, matching raw edges. Stitch, stretching neckband to fit. Finish raw edge of band.

10

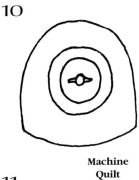

❖ Cut sliver of black felt and glue to face for nostril

❖ Cut plastic ball in half. Glue red satin fabric on ball. Glue covered ball to eye. Glue black felt ring around eye. Glue remaining felt eyepieces to ball.

11

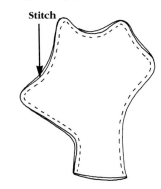

❖ Right sides facing out, sandwich lining, foam and fabric. Baste together along outside edge.

❖ Right sides together, pin and stitch another hand piece to foam sandwich. Stitch, trim and clip seams.

❖ Turn hand right side out.

❖ Machine quilt along marked lines on hand.

❖ Turn seam allowance along bottom to inside. Stitch in place.

See Photo on page 40.

FABRIC

4 yds. (3.7 m) Grey lightweight suede

1/2 yd. (46 cm) Pink lightweight suede

1/2 yd. (46 cm) Heavyweight iron-on interfacing

3 oz. Polyester fiberfill batting

NOTIONS

3' of 3-4" diam. (91 of 8-10 cm) Dryer vent hose

6'-7' of 1/2" O.D. (1.9-2.2 m of 1.3 cm) Flexible plastic tubing

12" (30.5 cm) Zipper

1 yd. (91 cm) Bias tape

Materials for papier-mâché (see *Chinese Dragon*)

SEAM ALLOWANCE

1/2" (1.3 cm)

1

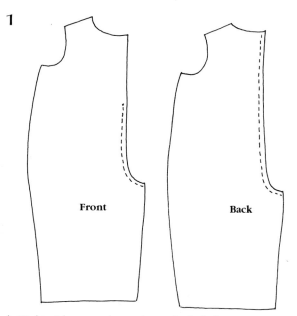

❖ Right sides together, pin and stitch front center seam as shown.

❖ Install zipper in front center seam, following manufacturer's instructions.

❖ Right sides together, stitch center back seam.

❖ Right sides together, stitch front to back at shoulder seams.

❖ Finish neck edge with bias tape.

2

❖ Right sides together, fold tail and stitch. Turn tail right side out and stuff. Hand stitch tail in place on back of costume.

❖ Ease stitch sleeves between notches.

❖ Right sides together, matching notches, stitch sleeves to front and back.

❖ Right sides together, stitch sleeve and side seams.

❖ Stitch inside leg seam.

❖ Narrow hem ends of sleeves and legs.

❖ Cut a strip of fabric 3" (7.6 cm) wide and the circumference of the body suit. Fold strip in half lengthwise, baste.

❖ On inside of body suit, stitch strip to dashed line. Leave opening to insert plastic tubing. Insert tubing to fill the circumference of waistline.

❖ Splice ends of plastic tubing together with tape.

3

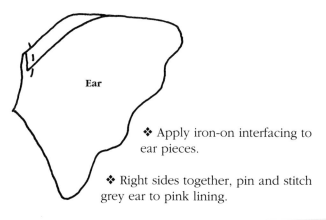

❖ Apply iron-on interfacing to ear pieces.

❖ Right sides together, pin and stitch grey ear to pink lining.

❖ Clip seams and turn right side out. Press.

❖ Turn top of ear down along fold line. Baste.

❖ Repeat for remaining ear.

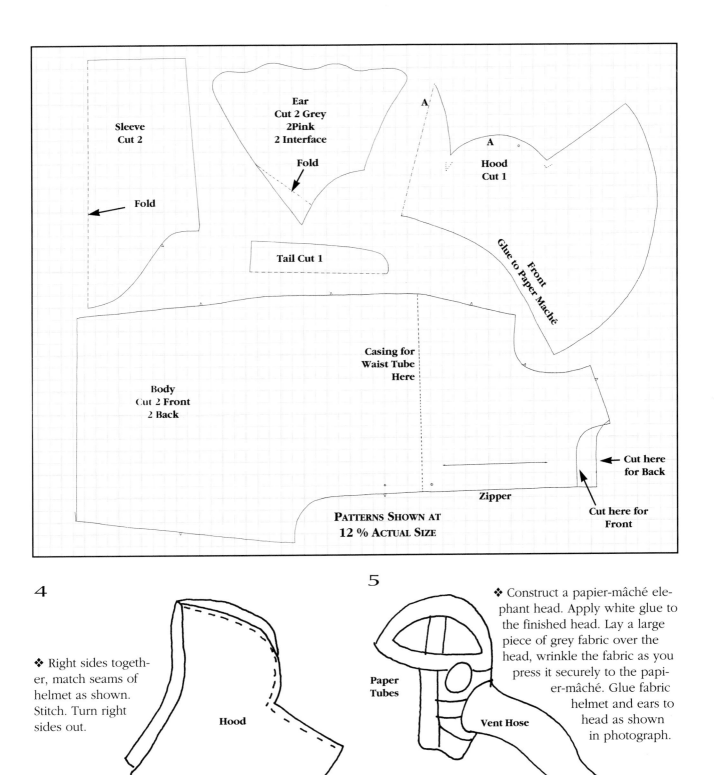

Sleeve Cut 2

Fold

Ear Cut 2 Grey 2Pink 2 Interface

Fold

A

A

Hood Cut 1

Tail Cut 1

Front Glue to Paper Mâché

Casing for Waist Tube Here

Body Cut 2 Front 2 Back

Cut here for Back

Zipper

PATTERNS SHOWN AT 12 % ACTUAL SIZE

Cut here for Front

4

❖ Right sides together, match seams of helmet as shown. Stitch. Turn right sides out.

Hood

5

Paper Tubes

Vent Hose

❖ Construct a papier-mâché elephant head. Apply white glue to the finished head. Lay a large piece of grey fabric over the head, wrinkle the fabric as you press it securely to the papier-mâché. Glue fabric helmet and ears to head as shown in photograph.

51

JUNGLE CAT

See Photo on page 41.

FABRIC

5 yds. (4.6 m) Yellow poly/cotton
1/8 yd. (11.4 cm) White poly/cotton
36" x 24" x 1/2" (91 x 61 x 1.3 cm.) Foam rubber
3 oz. Polyester fiberfill stuffing

**PATTERNS SHOWN AT
20 % ACTUAL SIZE**

NOTIONS

20" (51 cm) White zipper
Fabric paints (white, black, green)

SEAM ALLOWANCE

1/2" (1.3 cm)

Before construction, apply stripes to pattern pieces with fabric paint or markers.

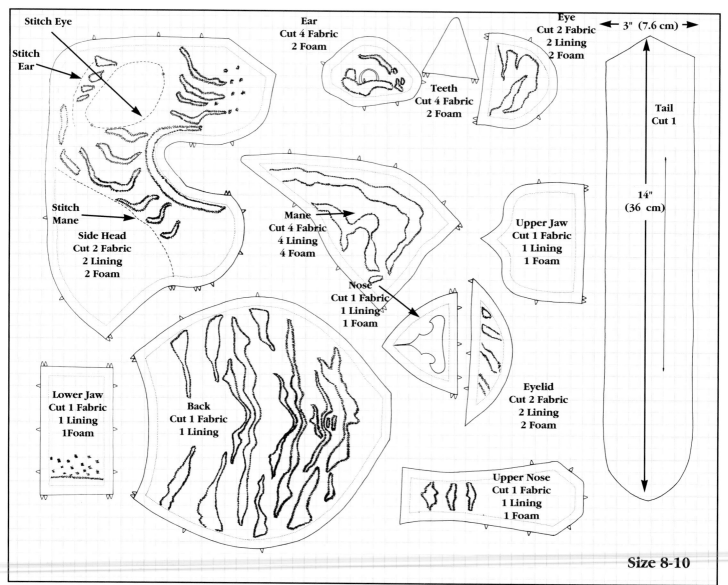

Pattern for the Jungle Cat. The pattern for the Jungle Cat's body suit appears on page 78.

1

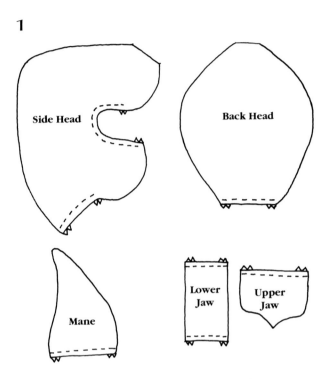

❖ Right sides together, pin and stitch the following pieces to their lining: right and left head, back head, mane (4 sets), lower jaw, upper jaw. Stitch from double notch to double notch as shown. Clip and trim seams.

❖ Turn pieces right side out and press.

❖ Insert matching foam pieces into fabric casings. Baste remaining seams closed.

2

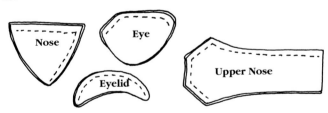

❖ Right sides facing out, pin and stitch the following pieces to their linings: nose, right and left eye, right and left eyelid, upper nose.

❖ Insert matching foam pieces. Baste remaining open seams closed.

3

❖ Right sides together, pin matching ear pieces. Stitch, leave opening between double notches. Trim, turn and press.

❖ Insert matching foam pieces into fabric casing. Turn under seam allowance.

❖ Baste opening closed.

❖ Repeat for remaining ear pieces.

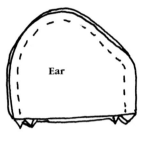

4

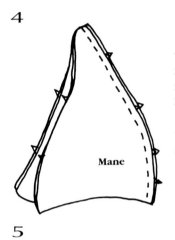

❖ Right sides together, matching notches, pin 2 mane pieces together. Stitch.

❖ Repeat for remaining mane pieces.

5

❖ Right sides together, pin 2 teeth pieces together. Stitch, leave opening between double notches. Trim and clip seam. Turn, right sides out. Stuff firmly with polyester fiberfill.

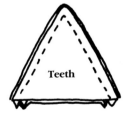

6

❖ Right sides together, match eyelid to eye, pin and stitch from A to B.

❖ Repeat for remaining eye and eyelid.

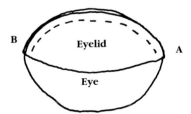

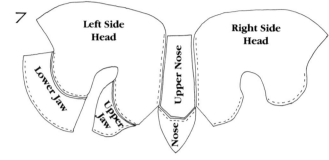

7

The mask is assembled by sequentially sewing pieces together. Refer to illustration. Right sides are faced together and seams are pinned, then stitched. Clip seams if necessary to aid in fit.

❖ Stitch nose to upper nose.

❖ Stitch left head to upper nose.

❖ Stitch left head to lower jaw.

❖ Stitch left head to upper jaw.

❖ Stitch right head to lower jaw.

❖ Stitch right head to upper jaw.

❖ Stitch right head to upper nose.

❖ Turn assembly right side out.

8

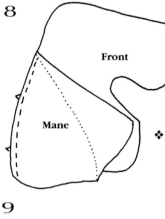

❖ Right sides facing up, place mane assembly on top of head, matching side seam, pin and stitch.

❖ Repeat for remaining side.

9

❖ Right sides together, pin back to side seams of right and left head. Pin and baste. Stitch.

❖ Turn assembly right side out.

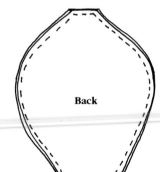

10

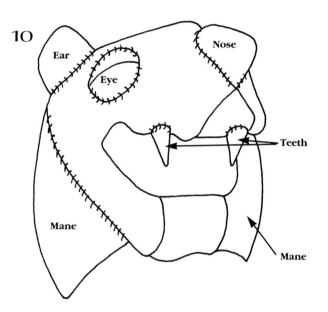

❖ Hand sew ears in place.

❖ Turn under seam allowance on mane and hand sew to side of head.

❖ Hand sew eyes in place.

❖ Hand sew teeth in place.

❖ Hand sew nose in place.

11

❖ Paint body suit pieces using photograph as a guide.

❖ Stitch body suit following directions for *Mummy.* *Note:* Do not stitch Mummy helmet. Use bias tape to bind neckline.

12

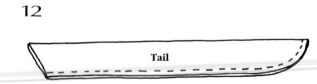

❖ Right sides together, fold tiger tail lengthwise. Pin and stitch. Turn tail right sides out. Stuff, and stitch to back of costume.

GORILLA IN A MONKEYSUIT

See Photo on page 42.

FABRIC

5/8 yd. of 54-60" (57 x 137-152 cm) Black
fake fur

1-1/2 yd. of 45" (137 x 114 cm) Black knit
for face and lining

1/8 yd. (11.4 cm) White felt for teeth

Scrap of black felt for nose

NOTIONS

36" x 18" (91.4 x 45.7 cm) of 1/2" (1.3 cm)
Thick foam rubber

6" of 1/2" (15.2 of 1.3 cm) Black hook and
loop tape

Two 19mm Safety eyes

ACCESSORIES

Tuxedo and dress shoes

SEAM ALLOWANCE

1/2" (1.3 cm)

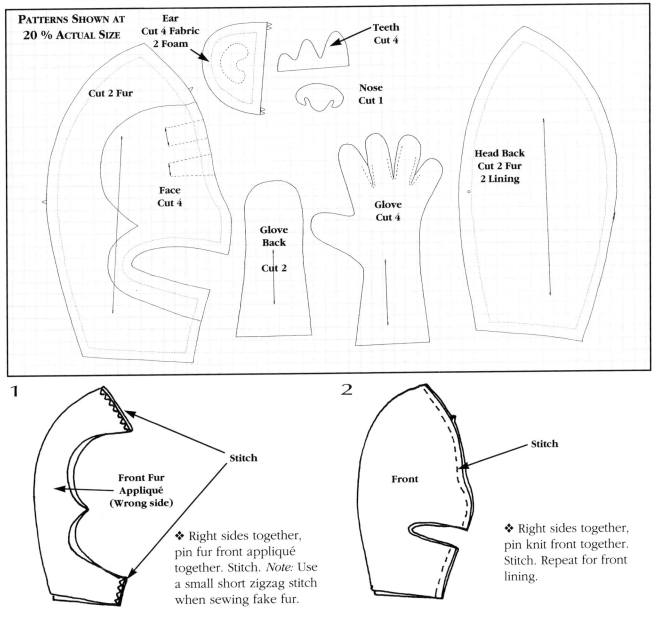

**PATTERNS SHOWN AT
20 % ACTUAL SIZE**

**Ear
Cut 4 Fabric
2 Foam**

**Teeth
Cut 4**

Cut 2 Fur

**Nose
Cut 1**

**Face
Cut 4**

**Glove
Back
Cut 2**

**Glove
Cut 4**

**Head Back
Cut 2 Fur
2 Lining**

1

Stitch

**Front Fur
Appliqué
(Wrong side)**

❖ Right sides together,
pin fur front appliqué
together. Stitch. *Note:* Use
a small short zigzag stitch
when sewing fake fur.

2

Stitch

Front

❖ Right sides together,
pin knit front together.
Stitch. Repeat for front
lining.

3

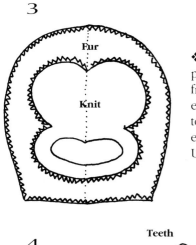

❖ Right sides facing up, pin front fur appliqué to front, match outside edges. Stitch pieces together along outside edges and inside curves. Use a small zigzag stitch.

4

❖ Pin two teeth felt pieces together along outside edge. Edgestitch as shown.

❖ Repeat for remaining teeth.

5

❖ Baste teeth to front face as shown.

6

❖ Right sides together, pin front lining to front at mouth area. Stitch. Clip curves and turn lining to inside. Press. Insert matching foam pieces into sides of head. Baste lining to front of head.

7

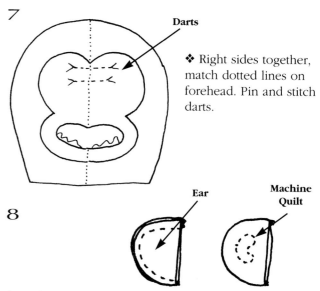

❖ Right sides together, match dotted lines on forehead. Pin and stitch darts.

8

❖ Right sides together, pin two ear pieces together. Stitch. Leave opening between double notches. Insert matching foam piece. Machine quilt along marked lines. Repeat for remaining ear.

9

❖ Baste ears to front head as shown.

10

❖ Right sides facing out, pin back to back lining as shown. Baste together. Repeat for remaining back and back lining.

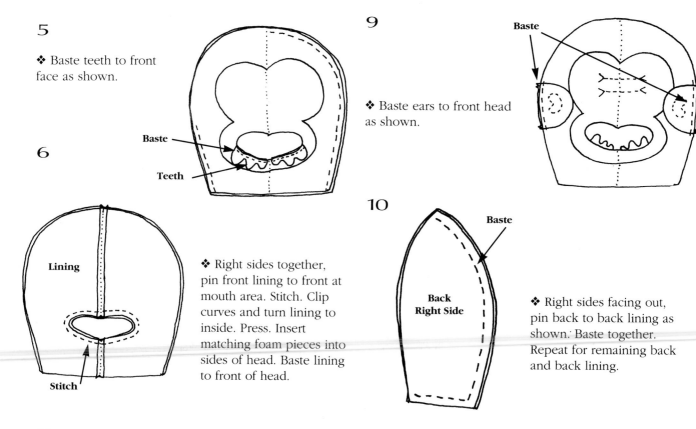

11

❖ Insert matching foam piece between lining and fabric. Baste opening closed.

12

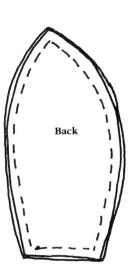

Back

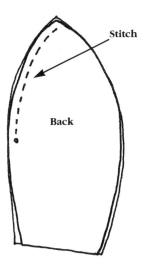

Stitch

Back

❖ Right sides together, pin back pieces together along center back seam. Stitch seam as shown. Stitch hook and loop tape to center back opening.

13

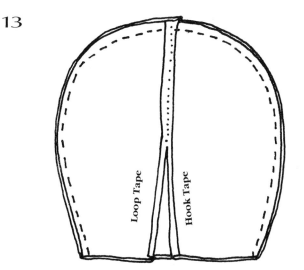

Loop Tape

Hook Tape

❖ Right sides together, pin front to back of mask. Stitch as shown.

❖ Turn up 1/2" (1.3 cm) along bottom seam to inside. Slip stitch to lining.

❖ Turn mask right side out.

❖ Following photograph, attach plastic eyes, stitch on felt nose.

❖ Cut thin strips of fake fur for eyebrows and hot glue in place.

14

❖ Use a seam allowance of 1/4" (6mm) for the gloves.

❖ Right sides facing up, appliqué fur to upper glove.

❖ Right sides together, pin applique glove upper half to plain glove lower half. Stitch, using a small zigzag stitch. Clip and trim seams. Turn glove right side out.

❖ Repeat for remaining glove.

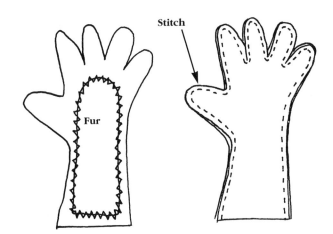

Stitch

Fur

MUNCHIE MADNESS

JUNKFOOD JUNKIE

See instructions on page 62.

Looks like this insatiable addict got a lot more than her hand caught in the cookie jar. When her mother said she could blow her whole allowance on an outfit, she never dreamed it would come to this!

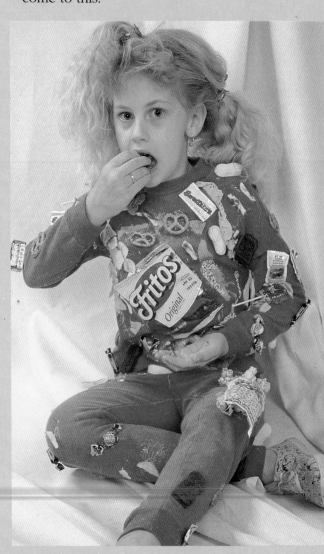

MEALS ON WHEELS

See instructions on page 62.

This may not be what the people at Social Services had in mind, but imagine the smiles she would bring to elderly shut-ins.

You are what you ate in this moving tribute to *haute couture* food packaging.

SOUR GRAPES

See instructions on page 62.

You'll have dizzying fun blowing up the balloons for this costume. And by the time the last balloon has popped like a champagne cork, your child will probably say, "I'm tired of being a bunch of grapes, anyway".

GINGERBREAD MAN'S REVENGE

See instructions on page 63.

How many times have we sacrificed these sweet little cookies unto the mouths of babes, who invariably bit their heads off first? Well, this G-Man is big, he's mean, and he's out for revenge. In short, he's one tough cookie!

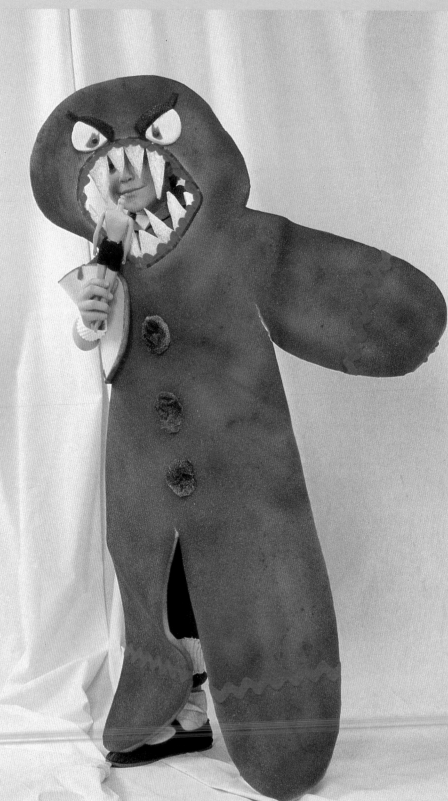

THE REFRIGERATOR

See instructions on page 64.

Decorated with magnets holding art and memos, it is itself a magnet to all civilized humans. A vault of snacks and goodies, what child wouldn't want to inhabit this tasty realm?

JUNKFOOD JUNKIE

See Photo on page 58.

MATERIALS

Old sweatsuit, preferably light in color
Candy, cookies, pretzels and chips
Hot glue and gun
Paint writers (red, yellow, brown)
Polyurethane sealant

❖ Start by spraying or dipping your junkfood in the polyurethane sealant as far in advance as possible, to give it plenty of time to dry properly. (Your exact drying times will be on the container itself.)

❖ Lay your sweatsuit flat. Put a piece of cardboard inside so that the sides don't stick together. You are now ready to start gluing your junkfood on. Just stick it anywhere. Let the child help, make it fun!

❖ You can use the paints for a mustard, ketchup and chocolate appearance, smearing them around.

MEALS ON WHEELS

See Photo on page 58.

MATERIALS

Leotard and tights, or sweatsuit
Roller skates
Empty food containers
Elastic, or plastic tape

❖ Simply attach food containers all over the foundation garment. Slits can be cut in boxes for elastic to pass through and fastened around limbs. Or, for an easier approach, plastic tape can be used. Either way, the color should match the foundation garment.

SOUR GRAPES

See Photo on page 59.

NOTIONS

60" (1.5 m) Wide twisted paper ribbon (green)
2–3 dozen 11" diam. (28 cm) Helium-type
    balloons (purple)
2–3 dozen Safety pins
3 12" (30.5 cm) Pipecleaners
2' of 1/2" wide (61 of 1.3 cm) Elastic
Green thread
Hot glue and gun

ACCESSORIES

Purple leotard and tights, or sweatsuit

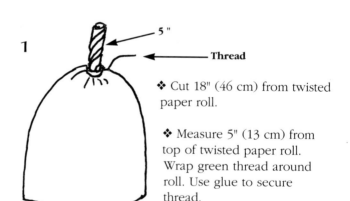

1

❖ Cut 18" (46 cm) from twisted paper roll.

❖ Measure 5" (13 cm) from top of twisted paper roll. Wrap green thread around roll. Use glue to secure thread.

❖ Open other end of the paper roll and turn up a 3-1/2" (9 cm) cuff to outside.

❖ Overlap end of elastic, glue.

❖ Place elastic circle inside cuff.

❖ Glue top of cuff every 1" (2.5 cm) to body of cap. This will keep the elastic from coming out of cuff.

2

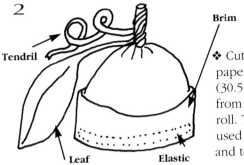

Tendril

Leaf Elastic Brim

❖ Cut a piece of paper 12" x 60" (30.5 x 152 cm) from remaining roll. This will be used to cut leaf and tendrils.

❖ Cut 2 leaf shapes. Hot glue a pipecleaner between the shapes.

❖ Glue a pipecleaner inside a piece of paper approx. 1" x 12" (2.5 x 30.5 cm). Twist into tendril shape.

❖ Following photograph, glue leaf and tendril onto cap.

3

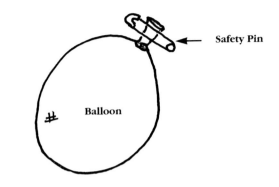

Safety Pin

Balloon

❖ Blow up and tie off balloons.

❖ Attach balloons to the leotard or sweatsuit with small safety pins.

GINGERBREAD MAN'S REVENGE

See Photo on page 60.

MATERIALS
3' x 4' x 1/2" (91 x 122 x 1.3 cm) Foam rubber,
   or other size to fit child
8' (2.4 m) Large red rickrack
2' (61 cm) Strand of red sequins
Pair of old socks and/or old T-shirt
1 yd. (91 cm) Ribbon or cord
Spray paint (brown)
Paints and brush (white, black)

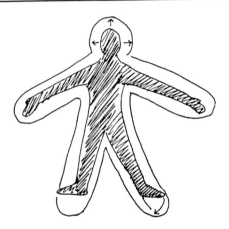

PATTERN
❖ Trace outline of child, lying down, onto a large sheet of paper—or directly onto the foam rubber. Enlarge this outline by a margin of 3" all the way around (see drawing).

❖ Draw features on pattern. Mouth extends from child's eyebrows to the chin. Draw "teeth" so as *not* to interfere with vision.

CUT
❖ Cut body pattern from foam rubber sheeting.

❖ Cut out mouth opening. *Note:* Teeth are cut as part of the body pattern. Clip edges of foam to shape and round the teeth.

❖ Cut eyes, eyebrows, and "raisin" buttons from foam scraps. Shape as desired.

PAINT
❖ Spray body brown. Paint teeth white.

❖ Paint eyes white, pupils of eyes black, eyebrows and "raisin" buttons black or a darker brown than you used on the body. Spray paint may be used or you can use an acrylic paint with a brush if you have it on hand. Set aside to dry. Wash out brush with soap and water.

Optional: Hold can of gold spray paint 12"-14" (30-36 cm) from surface and *mist* lightly across the body and raisins for a "sugared" effect.

ASSEMBLE

❖ When dry, glue eyes, eyebrows and "raisins" on body of costume using foam adhesive. Follow instructions on can for best results.

DECORATE

❖ Glue giant rickrack on arms and legs. For mouth, fold rickrack in half lengthwise and glue around the mouth opening. Glue one row of single strand sequins around outside of mouth.

STRAPS

❖ Cut 4 straps out of old socks (men's white athletic socks work well for this). Glue these strips on the back

of the costume at the wrist position using foam adhesive. Repeat for the ankle straps. *Note:* Insert a paper or cardboard barrier between the layer of sock before pressing into place to preserve the opening. Cut a long cord or ribbon and glue 2" (5 cm) of the center of this cord to the forehead position on back of costume.

❖ If additional support is desired for the body, glue a T-shirt to the back of the costume using the same technique as described for the "sock" straps.

THE REFRIGERATOR

See Photo on page 61.

MATERIALS

    12" x 17" x 24" (31 x 43 x 61 cm) Corrugated
        cardboard box
    1/2" x 4' x 4' (1.3 x 122 x 122 cm) Foam core
    insulation board with foil on one side
    Duct tape, black tape, white tape, decorative
        colored tape, double-sided tape
    Heavy aluminum foil
    White spray enamel, 2 cans
    Decorative paint
    White glue
    2 pieces of wire, approximately 12" (31 cm)
        and 3" (8 cm) long
    1 round shank button
    Sticky-back hook and loop tape, 2" (5 cm) strip

1

❖ Open one end of the box and tape flaps to the inside.

2

❖ From the foam board, cut 2 sides the height of the box x the depth plus 6" (15 cm). Glue and tape the sides to the box, foil side in, with the top, bottom, and back flush with the box and the excess extending to the front.

❖ Cut the top to the width of the box with the sides attached and the same depth as the sides. Don't attach the top yet, but put it in place and measure for the door. Cut the door the outer dimensions of the front opening.

❖ For the bottom front and inside shelf, cut 2 pieces of foam board the length of the interior front width measurement and the width of the interior front depth measurement minus 1/2" (1.3 cm).

3

❖ Glue aluminum foil to the upper half of the inner front compartment. Tape the shelf in place, foil side up, about halfway down from the top of the inner compartment. Tape the remaining rectangle in place at the bottom of the front compartment.

❖ From the foam board, cut a door for the inner front compartment. Cut to the inner dimensions of the lower front section, below the shelf. Cut this piece in half horizontally. Spray paint the pieces. Abut the cut edges and tape together on the painted side with white tape to form a hinge. Mark a point about halfway along one long edge and 1" (2.5 cm) from the edge. Run the shorter piece of wire through the button shank, then put both ends through the door at the marked point. Fold the ends flat on the inside of the door and tape over them.

❖ Position the door in the lower front opening, the half with the knob upward and flush with the shelf. Tape in place, taping the lower half only and keeping the upper half free. Pull the upper half open to horizontal position and put a strip of tape across the joint on the inside. Tape the cut edges of the upper door with white tape.

4

❖ For door handle, cut 2 pieces of foam board 1" x 6" (2.5 x 15.2 cm). Glue them together, one on top of the other, to make 1 piece 1" x 6" x 1" thick. Hold the handle in position on the outside of the refrigerator door and make a hole through the handle and door near each end of the handle. Run the ends of the longer wire through the holes to the inside of the door. Fold the ends of the wire flat and tape in place with duct tape. Cover the handle with black tape.

❖ Tape the refrigerator top in place. Position the door on front. On the outside, tape the door to the box along one long edge. Open the door and tape the same edge on the inside. Attach sticky-back hook and loop tape to the open front edge of the refrigerator and to the corresponding spot on the inside of the door. Close the door and spray paint the refrigerator.

5

❖ For cookie jar, cut 8 strips of foam board 12" x 4" (30.5 x 10.2 cm). Cut a circle 12" in diameter. Lay the rectangular pieces side by side with long edges abutting and foil sides up. Tape the pieces together to form a strip. Spray paint the circle and the untaped side of the strip. Cover the edge of the circle with decorative tape.

❖ Cut circular holes in the refrigerator for child's head and arms. On top, cut a hole for the head approximately 8-1/2" (21.6 cm) in diameter, placing the center of the circle 6" (15.2 cm) from the back of the box and center it between the sides. For the arms, cut a hole approximately 5" (12.7 cm) in diameter, with the center of the circle 5" from the top of the box and 6" from the back. Cover the cut edges of the arm holes with white tape.

❖ Have the child try on the refrigerator. Place the cookie jar strip around the child's head and mark positions of the eyes, probably about 6" (15 cm) up and 2-1/2" (6.4 cm) apart. Paint the word "cookies" on the strip, with the Os at the marked eye positions. Cut the centers of the Os.

❖ Using a round plate or bowl as a form, tape the ends of the cookie jar strip together, on the inside, to form a cylinder. Center it over the hole on top of the refrigerator and tape in place from the inside. Tape outside joints with decorative tape. Glue the lid on top of the jar. For the knob, cover a small section of cardboard tube or a thread spool with decorative tape and glue to the lid.

6

❖ Finishing details: Put empty, lightweight food containers on the refrigerator shelf, keeping them in place with double-sided tape. Tape refrigerator magnets, shopping lists, artwork, etc., to the door. Paint a label, "treats," and tape it to the door of the inner compartment.

THE DARK SIDE

WEIRD WARLOCK

See instructions on page 76.

When it comes to a little dabbling in that old black magic, there's no reason why the girls should have all the fun. Just as a story wouldn't be nearly as fascinating without a villain, children need to explore their dark side. This simple costume offers a safe and fun way to conjure up a little mischief.

WICKED WITCH

See instructions on page 73.

Witches have become synonymous with Halloween, and sooner or later your child will probably want to be one. Who can resist the somber, mismatched garb, the crumpled hat and striped stockings, long nails, wild hair, warts and wrinkles...or the urge to cast spells!

The Mummy

See instructions on page 78.

Was this Egyptian mummy's boy so tightly wrapped he's reawakened from the dead? Or is this some poor child who has a devil of a time getting untangled from his bed sheets every morning?

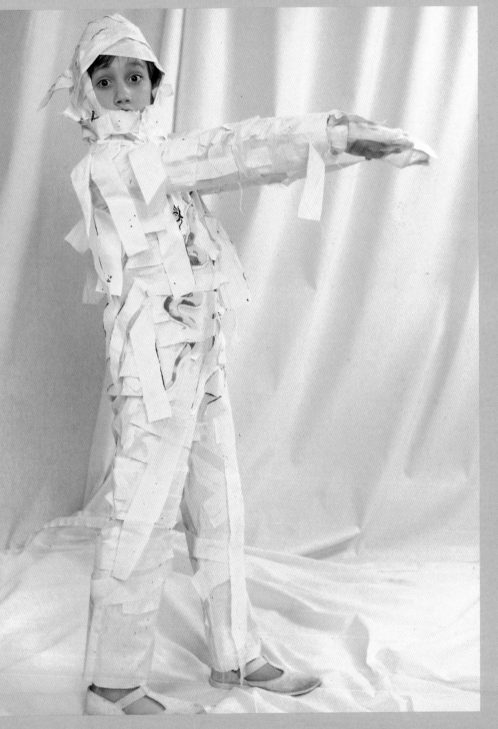

MUSCLE MANIAC

See instructions on page 80.

Natural athleticism is one thing, but this big bully is obviously a result of gymnastic excess. Pump it, flex it—no pain, no gain. Pretty scary, huh?

DREADED COCKROACH

See instructions on page 81.

Cockroaches have been around 350 million years—much longer than dinosaurs. They are truly creatures of the night. If you go to the kitchen to pour yourself a latenight drink and forget to turn on the light, you'd better hope there isn't a cockroach waiting for you in the bottom of your cup…gulp!

THE CYCLOPS

See instructions on page 86.

The cyclops is described in ancient legends as a fierce one-eyed giant that likes to eat people. Actually, someone long ago may have discovered an elephant skull and mistook the large trunk hole as an eye socket. The "two left feet" theory is still in question.

BOG MONSTER

See instructions on page 90.

Deep in the Black Lagoon, there is a cave. This is the home of the Bog Monster, who never takes a bath and never ever brushes his teeth. He eats only bugs and snakes, unless some tasty child wanders too far into the bog.

CHINESE DRAGON

See instructions on page 92.

This dragon makes a very dramatic appearance in every Chinese New Year parade. Even though the largest child wears the head, anyone who tags along gets to create a winding, larger-than-life serpent.

See Photo on page 66.

You and your child can have a lot of fun improvising this costume from recycled clothing and scraps. Search your closets, ask your neighbors, browse the thrift stores and rummage sales for anything that strikes your fancy. Even colors don't matter because you can dip the entire costume in black or navy blue dye when you're finished.

Using your child as a mannequin, you can cut, layer, pin and baste the various parts together. To aid in the final fit, add a casing to the waist area and thread 1/2" (1.3 cm) elastic through the casing to fit the waist measurement. A kitchen curtain was cut into a triangle for this shawl. A nylon net slip was shredded, and the polka dot skirt was draped into a bustle.

No doubt, you'll create your own version, and may want to add a few other touches: like a cloak and a broom. Here's how to make the hat.

FABRIC

22" x 15" (56 x 38 cm) Black felt
45" x 36" (114 x 91 cm) Navy blue taffeta
40" x 20" (102 x 51 cm) Iron-on interfacing

SEAM ALLOWANCE

1/2" (1.3 cm)

1

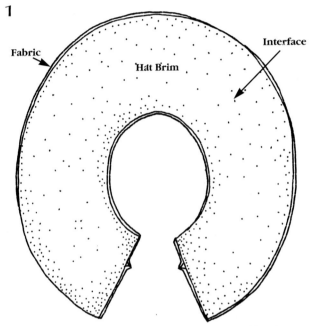

❖ Apply iron-on interfacing to wrong side of hat brim and hat brim lining.

2

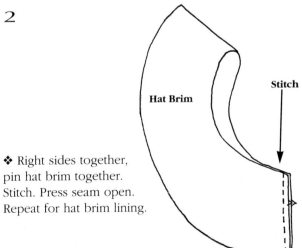

❖ Right sides together, pin hat brim together. Stitch. Press seam open. Repeat for hat brim lining.

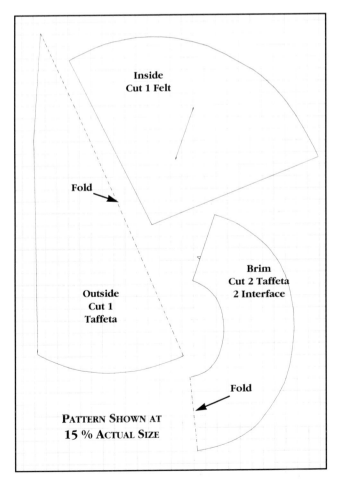

Inside
Cut 1 Felt

Fold

Outside
Cut 1
Taffeta

Brim
Cut 2 Taffeta
2 Interface

Fold

PATTERN SHOWN AT
15 % ACTUAL SIZE

3

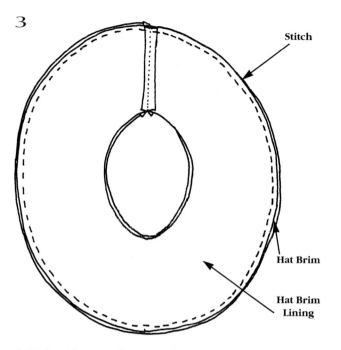

Stitch

Hat Brim

Hat Brim
Lining

❖ Right sides together, matching seams, pin hat brim to hat brim lining. Stitch along outside edge. Trim seam and turn hat brim right side out. Press.

4

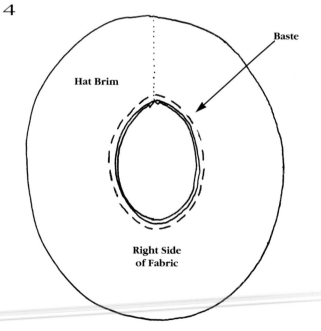

Baste

Hat Brim

Right Side
of Fabric

❖ Baste raw edges of hat brim together. Stitch brim of hat as shown.

5

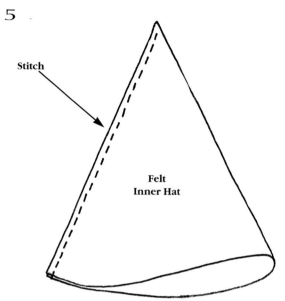

Stitch

Felt
Inner Hat

❖ Right sides together, pin and stitch inner felt hat as shown. Press seam open.

6

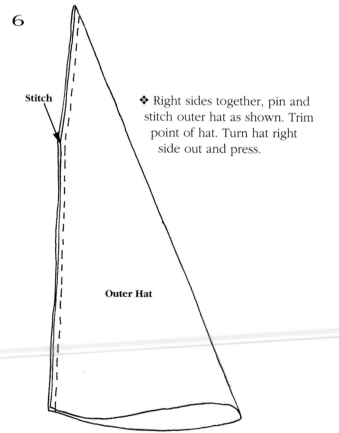

Stitch

Outer Hat

❖ Right sides together, pin and stitch outer hat as shown. Trim point of hat. Turn hat right side out and press.

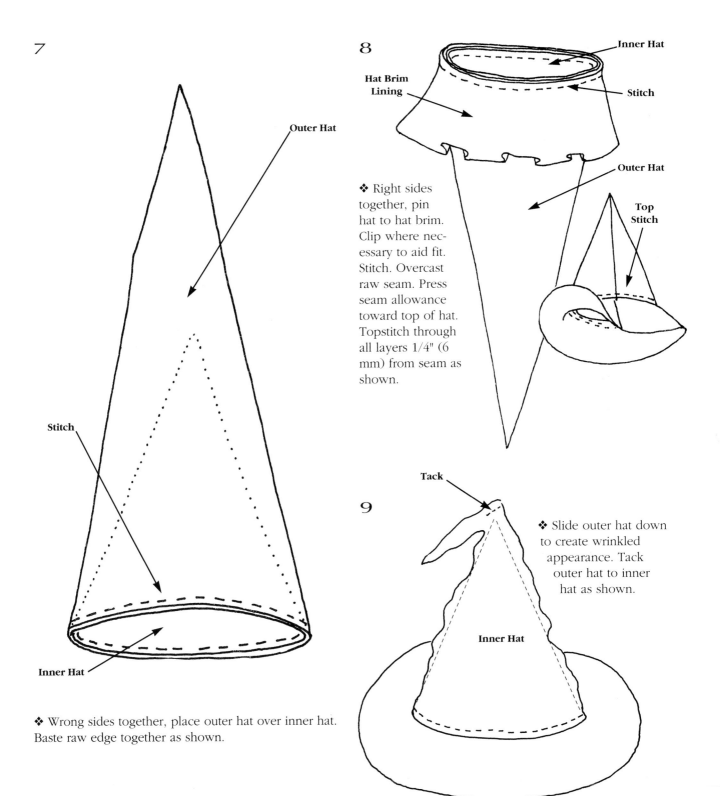

7

Outer Hat

Stitch

Inner Hat

❖ Wrong sides together, place outer hat over inner hat. Baste raw edge together as shown.

8

Inner Hat

Hat Brim Lining

Stitch

Outer Hat

Top Stitch

❖ Right sides together, pin hat to hat brim. Clip where necessary to aid fit. Stitch. Overcast raw seam. Press seam allowance toward top of hat. Topstitch through all layers 1/4" (6 mm) from seam as shown.

9

Tack

Inner Hat

❖ Slide outer hat down to create wrinkled appearance. Tack outer hat to inner hat as shown.

See Photo on page 66.

FABRIC

2 yds. (1.8 m) Black poly/cotton
5/8 yd. (57 cm) Silver lamé
1/8 yd. (11.4 cm) Felt

NOTIONS

1/2 yd. (46 cm) Heavyweight iron-on
    interfacing
3 oz. Polyester fiberfill stuffing
1/2 yd. (46 cm) Polyester fiberfill batting
2 sets of 1/2" (1.3 cm) Hook and loop dots
Hot glue and glue gun

ACCESSORIES

Black or dark play clothes
Mystical pendant on necklace
Black hat (see instructions for *Maid Marian*)

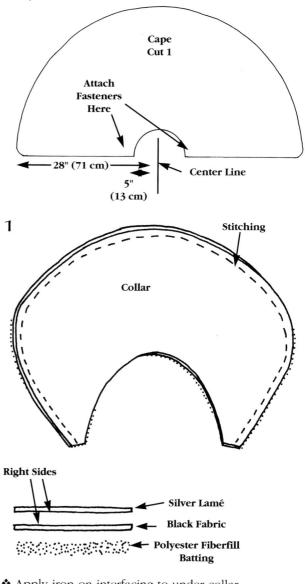

1

❖ Apply iron-on interfacing to under collar.

❖ Make a sandwich of collars (right sides together, and polyester fiberfill batting).

❖ Pin collar together and stitch.

❖ Clip and trim seams. Turn right side out.

❖ Baste raw edges of collar together.

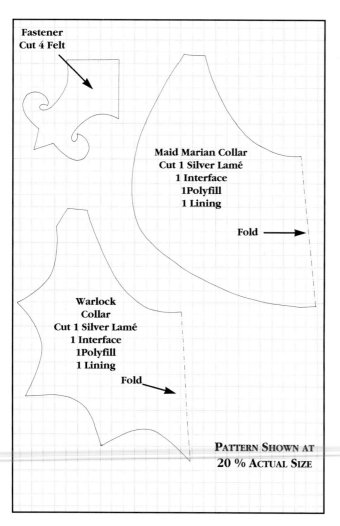

2

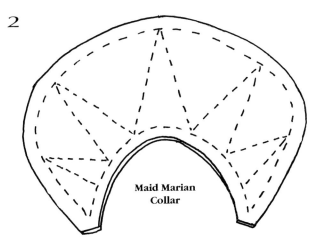

Maid Marian Collar

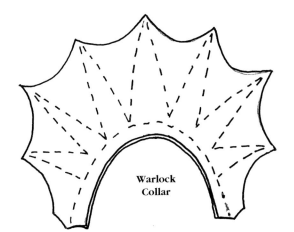

Warlock Collar

❖ Machine quilt as shown by dotted lines.

3

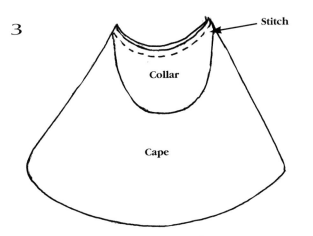

Stitch

Collar

Cape

❖ Finish side and bottom edges of cape.

❖ Place under collar facing right side of cape.

❖ Matching center back, pin collar to cape. Pin. Stitch.

❖ Press seam toward cape. Serge or zigzag to finish edge.

❖ Stitch through cape and seam.

4

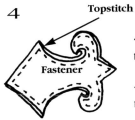

Topstitch

Fastener

❖ Glue or topstitch two fasteners together.

❖ Hot glue hook and loop dots to fasteners.

5

❖ Stitch or glue felt fasteners to cape.

See Photo on page 67.

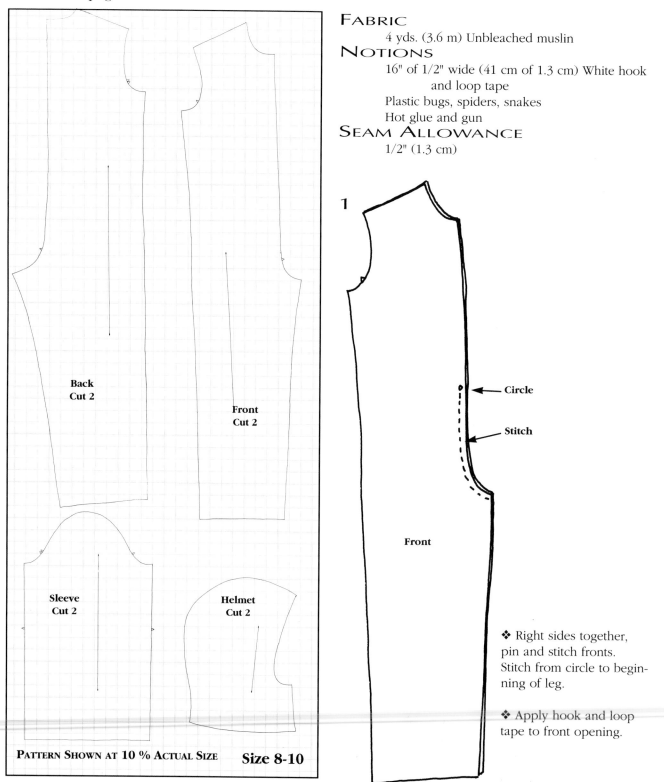

Back
Cut 2

Front
Cut 2

Sleeve
Cut 2

Helmet
Cut 2

PATTERN SHOWN AT 10 % ACTUAL SIZE **Size 8-10**

FABRIC
4 yds. (3.6 m) Unbleached muslin
NOTIONS
16" of 1/2" wide (41 cm of 1.3 cm) White hook
and loop tape
Plastic bugs, spiders, snakes
Hot glue and gun
SEAM ALLOWANCE
1/2" (1.3 cm)

1

← Circle

← Stitch

Front

❖ Right sides together, pin and stitch fronts. Stitch from circle to beginning of leg.

❖ Apply hook and loop tape to front opening.

2

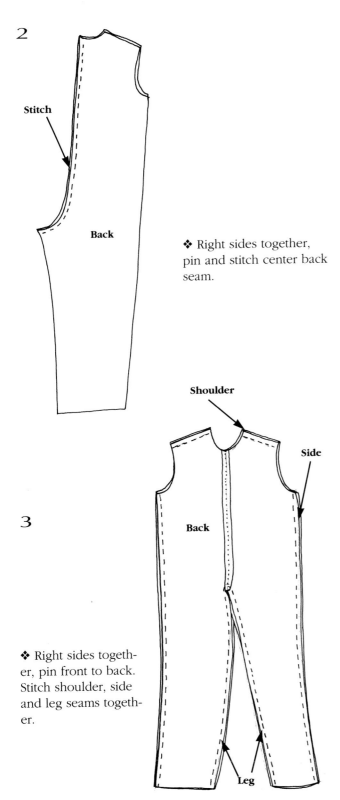

Stitch

Back

❖ Right sides together, pin and stitch center back seam.

4

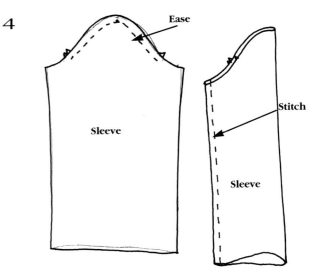

Ease

Sleeve

Stitch

Sleeve

❖ Ease stitch sleeve between notches.

❖ Right sides together, pin and stitch sleeve seam.

❖ Right sides together, matching notches, pin sleeve to armhole. Pin and stitch.

❖ Repeat for remaining sleeve. Narrow hem pants and sleeves.

Shoulder

Back

Side

3

Leg

❖ Right sides together, pin front to back. Stitch shoulder, side and leg seams together.

5

❖ Right sides together, pin and stitch hood as shown.

❖ Right sides together, pin and stitch hood to jump suit.

❖ Cut or tear strips of muslin 1-1/2" (4 cm) wide. Hot glue strips to costume. Use photo as a guide.

❖ Splash costume with brown fabric paint. Glue or stitch plastic spiders and snakes to fabric.

Stitch

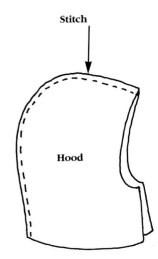

Hood

See Photo on page 68.

Fabric

3 yds. of 60" wide (2.7 m of 152 cm) Flesh-
colored double-knit poly/cotton
1/4 yd. (23 cm) Spandex (bikini)

Notions

Loose pack fiberfill
18" (46 cm) Zipper

1

❖ Cut each pattern piece *twice* from doubled fabric, placing the pattern pieces with the grainline on the lengthwise grain of the fabric.

2

❖ Sew all pieces with right sides together and with 1/4" (6 mm) seams.

❖ Make the outer suit. Sew the front pieces together along the center front from crotch to neckline. Sew back pieces together along center back from crotch to the notch at the lower end of the zipper. Machine baste the remainder of the seam to the neckline. Press seam open.

❖ Center the zipper, face down, over the basted portion of the back seam. Baste one side of the zipper tape to the seam allowance only, keeping the back free. Stitch. Then stitch along both sides of the zipper through all thicknesses.

❖ Stitch across the bottom of the zipper just below the stop. Remove basting.

❖ Stitch sleeve fronts to front of suit, matching notches. Stitch sleeve backs to back of suit. Stitch back of suit to front along sides and under sleeves. Stitch inner leg seam from ankle to ankle.

3

❖ Make the inner suit in the same manner, leaving center back seam open above the notch.

❖ Put the inner suit into the outer suit with *wrong* sides together. Turn center back seam allowance of inner suit to the inside along the zipper and stitch in place. Stitch layers together at neck, wrists, and ankles, using a zigzag stitch.

4

❖ Have the child try on the suit. With musclemen magazine photos as a guide, draw muscles on the suit with a fabric marker. Stitch by hand along the marked lines, stretching the fabric while stitching to keep the stitching very loose. Carefully cut a slit, through the inner suit fabric only, at the center of each "muscle." Stuff each with fiberfill and stitch the openings.

5

❖ To make the bikini, cut one back and one front. Stitch the crotch seam. Try the bikini on the child over the muscle suit and pin the side seams. Stitch the sides. Stitch a narrow hem around the leg openings and around the top with a zigzag stitch.

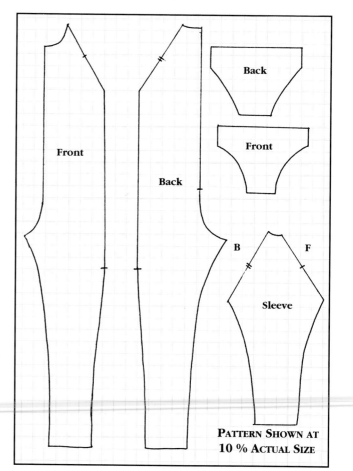

Front

Back

Back

Front

B   F

Sleeve

PATTERN SHOWN AT 10 % ACTUAL SIZE

DREADED COCKROACH

See Photo on page 69.

FABRIC

- 18" x 6" (45.7 x 15.2 cm) Black felt
- 2-1/2 yds. of 45" (2.3 m x 114 cm) Brown moire taffeta
- 1 yd. of 45" (92 x 114 cm) Navy blue taffeta
- 5/8 yd. of 36" (57.2 x 92 cm) Blue netting
- 5/8 yd. (57.2 cm) Iron-on interfacing
- 26" x 12" (66 x 30.5 cm) Polyester fiberfill batting
- 36" x 24" x 1/2" (91.4 x 61 x 1.3 cm) Foam sheeting

NOTIONS

- 3" (7.6 cm) Plastic ball
- 2-1/4" (5.7 cm) O.D. x 18" (45.7 cm) Plastic tube
- 5" of 1/2" (12.7 of 1.3 cm) Hook and loop tape
- 12" (30.5 cm) Single-fold black bias tape
- 1-3/4 yd. of 1/2" (1.5 m of 1.3 cm) Black grosgrain ribbon

ACCESSORIES

- Black gloves
- Black turtleneck and tights
- Black shoes and socks

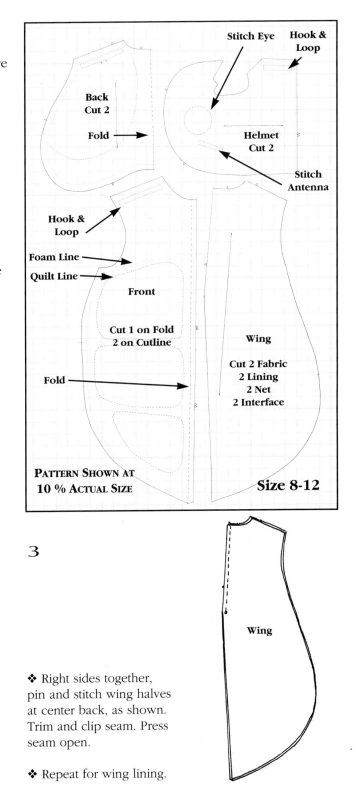

1

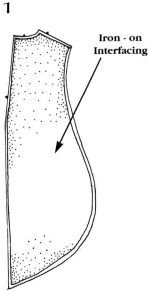

Iron - on Interfacing

❖ Fuse iron-on interfacing to wrong side of wings.

2

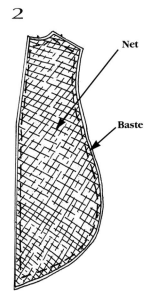

Net

Baste

❖ Place net wings onto right side of wings, pin and baste.

3

❖ Right sides together, pin and stitch wing halves at center back, as shown. Trim and clip seam. Press seam open.

❖ Repeat for wing lining.

Wing

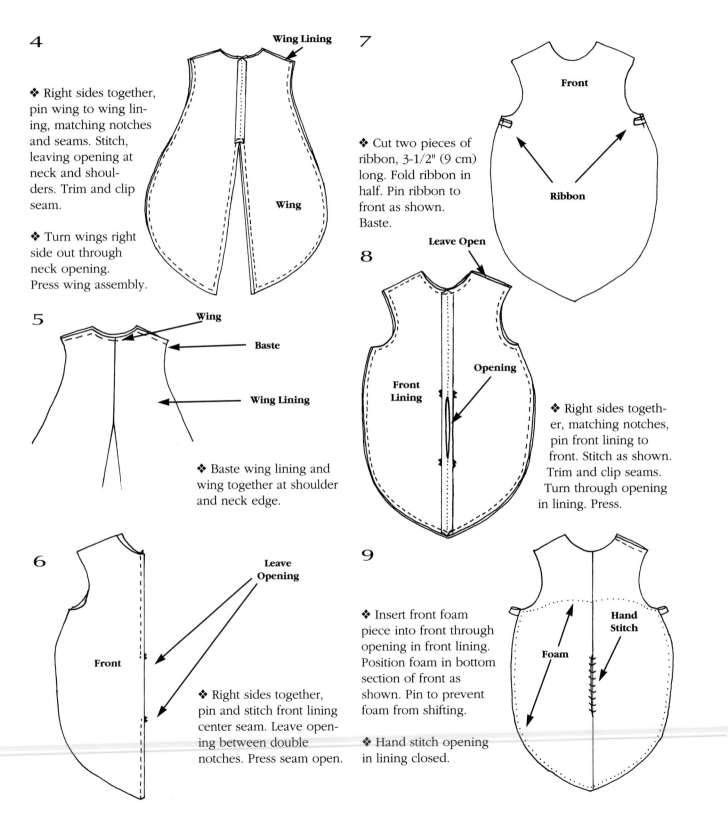

4

❖ Right sides together, pin wing to wing lining, matching notches and seams. Stitch, leaving opening at neck and shoulders. Trim and clip seam.

❖ Turn wings right side out through neck opening. Press wing assembly.

Wing Lining

Wing

5

Wing

Baste

Wing Lining

❖ Baste wing lining and wing together at shoulder and neck edge.

6

Leave Opening

Front

❖ Right sides together, pin and stitch front lining center seam. Leave opening between double notches. Press seam open.

7

Front

Ribbon

❖ Cut two pieces of ribbon, 3-1/2" (9 cm) long. Fold ribbon in half. Pin ribbon to front as shown. Baste.

8

Leave Open

Front Lining

Opening

❖ Right sides together, matching notches, pin front lining to front. Stitch as shown. Trim and clip seams. Turn through opening in lining. Press.

9

Hand Stitch

Foam

❖ Insert front foam piece into front through opening in front lining. Position foam in bottom section of front as shown. Pin to prevent foam from shifting.

❖ Hand stitch opening in lining closed.

10

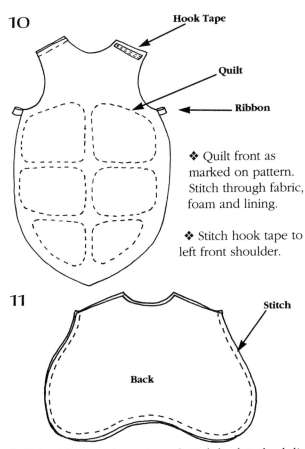

Hook Tape

Quilt

Ribbon

❖ Quilt front as marked on pattern. Stitch through fabric, foam and lining.

❖ Stitch hook tape to left front shoulder.

11

Stitch

Back

❖ Right sides together, pin and stitch back to back lining. Trim and clip seam.

❖ Turn through opening in neck. Press.

❖ Insert foam between back and back lining.

12

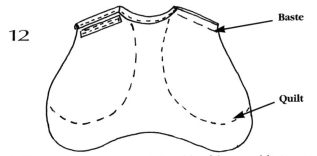

Baste

Quilt

❖ Pin and baste neck and shoulder fabric and lining as shown.

❖ Quilt as marked on pattern. Stitching through fabric, foam and lining.

13

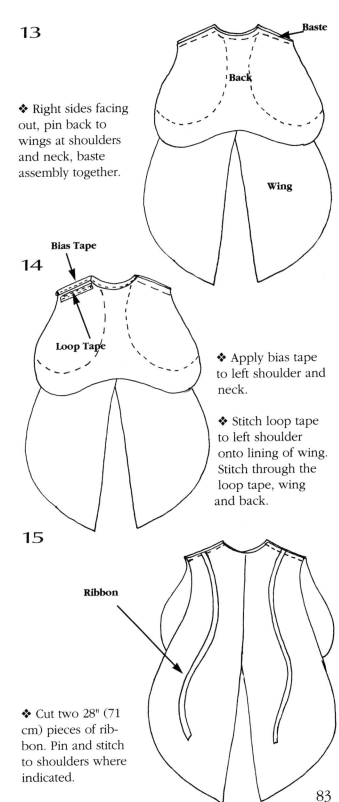

Baste

Back

Wing

❖ Right sides facing out, pin back to wings at shoulders and neck, baste assembly together.

14

Bias Tape

Loop Tape

❖ Apply bias tape to left shoulder and neck.

❖ Stitch loop tape to left shoulder onto lining of wing. Stitch through the loop tape, wing and back.

15

Ribbon

❖ Cut two 28" (71 cm) pieces of ribbon. Pin and stitch to shoulders where indicated.

83

16

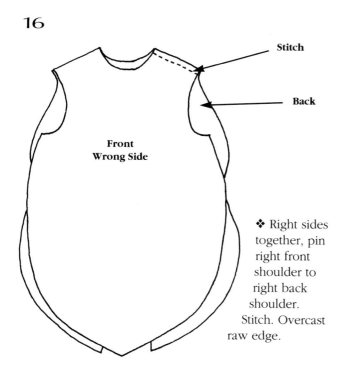

Stitch

Back

**Front
Wrong Side**

❖ Right sides together, pin right front shoulder to right back shoulder. Stitch. Overcast raw edge.

17

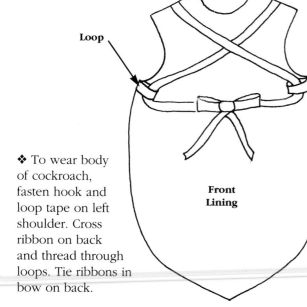

Loop

**Front
Lining**

❖ To wear body of cockroach, fasten hook and loop tape on left shoulder. Cross ribbon on back and thread through loops. Tie ribbons in bow on back.

18

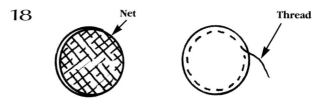

Net

Thread

❖ Cut two 3" (7.6 cm) circles from blue taffeta and a matching pair of circles from blue net for eyes.

❖ Baste a net circle to a fabric circle. Gather outside edge of circle.

19

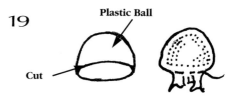

Plastic Ball

Cut

❖ Cut plastic ball in half, using a utility knife.

❖ Place half of ball in center of fabric circle, pull gathering threads to fit. Fasten threads securely and tuck seam allowances to inside of ball.

❖ Repeat for remaining eye.

20

❖ Baste batting to wrong side of helmet pieces.

❖ Right sides together, pin and stitch center seam of helmet. Trim and clip seams.

❖ Repeat for helmet lining.

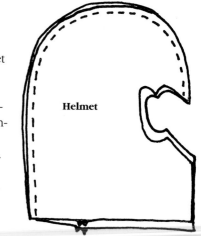

Helmet

21

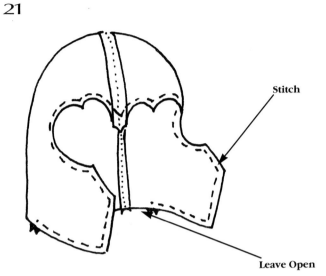

Stitch

Leave Open

❖ Right sides together, pin and stitch helmet to helmet lining. Leave opening between double notches.

❖ Trim and clip seams. Turn right side out through opening. Press.

❖ Turn seam allowance in opening to inside. Hand stitch opening closed.

❖ Top stitch around outer edge of helmet.

❖ Apply hook and loop tape to front of helmet as shown on pattern.

22

❖ Fold black felt around plastic tube. Use a zipper foot stitch close to plastic tube. Trim seam very close.

❖ Repeat for remaining antenna.

23

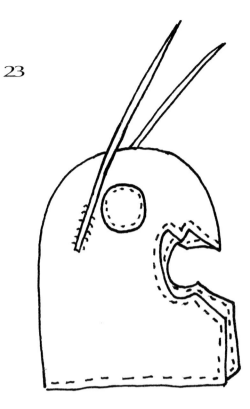

❖ Hand stitch antenna to position marked on helmet.

❖ Hand stitch eyes to helmet.

See Photo on page 70.

FABRIC

1/8 yd. (12 cm) White fabric
12" x 24" (30 x 61 cm) Brown imitation leather
1 yd. (91 cm) Fake fur
1-1/2 yd. (137 cm) Brown poly/cotton
1 yd. (91 cm) Olive green poly/cotton
6" x 6" (15 x 15 cm) Yellow knit
36" x 2" (92 x 5 cm) Purple knit

NOTIONS

3" (7.6 cm) Plastic ball
19 mm Safety eye
1 yd. (91 cm) Bias tape
2 packages Brown baby rickrack
1 yd. of 1/2" (91 of 1.3 cm) Foam rubber
Pair of shoulder pads
Dried chicken bone

SEAM ALLOWANCE

1/2" (1.3 cm)

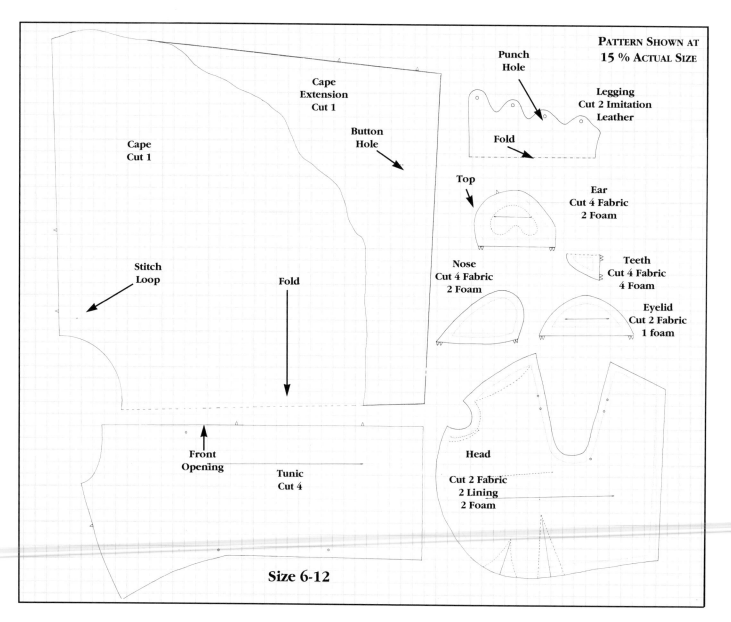

PATTERN SHOWN AT 15 % ACTUAL SIZE

Cape Extension Cut 1

Punch Hole

Legging Cut 2 Imitation Leather

Fold

Button Hole

Cape Cut 1

Top

Ear Cut 4 Fabric 2 Foam

Nose Cut 4 Fabric 2 Foam

Teeth Cut 4 Fabric 4 Foam

Eyelid Cut 2 Fabric 1 foam

Stitch Loop

Fold

Front Opening

Tunic Cut 4

Head Cut 2 Fabric 2 Lining 2 Foam

Size 6-12

1

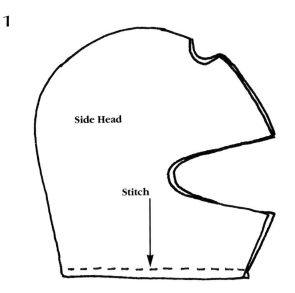

Side Head

Stitch

❖ Right sides together, pin and stitch bottom seam of right side of head and head lining together.

❖ Turn head pieces, right side facing out, and press.

2

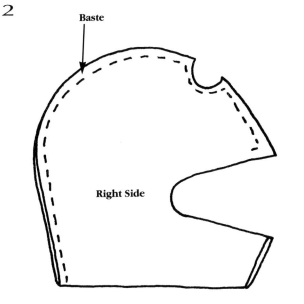

Baste

Right Side

❖ Pin head to head lining and baste as shown.

3

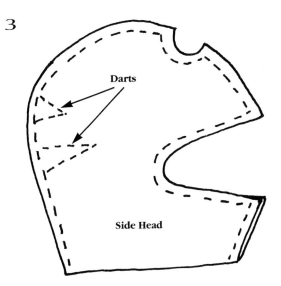

Darts

Side Head

❖ Insert matching foam piece between head and head lining piece.

❖ Pin, stitch remaining open seams.

❖ Pin and stitch darts.

❖ Repeat for remaining head piece.

4

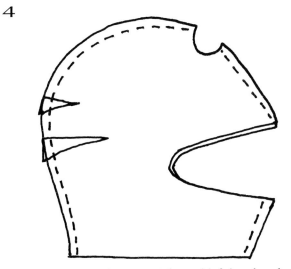

❖ Right sides together, pin right and left head and stitch as shown.

❖ Turn head right sides out.

5

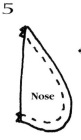

❖ Right sides facing out, stitch nose to nose lining. Leave open between double notches. Insert matching foam piece. Baste opening closed.

❖ Repeat for remaining nose pieces.

❖ Right sides together, pin two nose pieces together. Stitch, leaving opening between double notches.

6

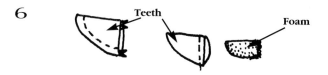

❖ Right sides together, pin and stitch two teeth pieces. Leave opening between double notches.

❖ Trim seams, turn and press.

❖ Insert matching foam piece.

❖ Turn seam allowance to inside and baste opening closed.

7

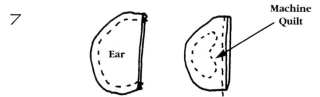

❖ Repeat procedure for teeth to make ears and eyelid. *Note:* Machine quilt ears as indicated on pattern.

8

❖ Cut 1/4 of plastic ball as shown, discard.

❖ Place plastic ball on circle of fabric.

❖ Gather raw edge of fabric. Secure fabric to ball.

❖ Insert plastic eye into the center of plastic ball.

9

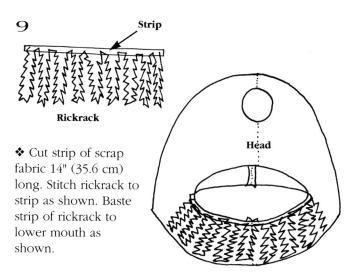

❖ Cut strip of scrap fabric 14" (35.6 cm) long. Stitch rickrack to strip as shown. Baste strip of rickrack to lower mouth as shown.

11

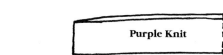

❖ Cut strip of knit fabric 36" x 2" (92 x 5 cm).

❖ Right sides together, stitch short side of mouth together. Fold strip in half and baste raw edges together.

12

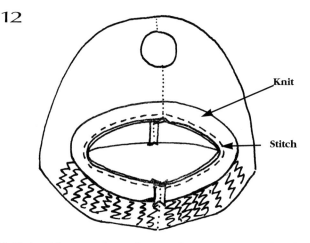

❖ Right sides together, pin mouth to opening in head, baste.

❖ Turn mouth to inside. Cover raw edge with folded edge of knit fabric. Hand stitch in place.

13

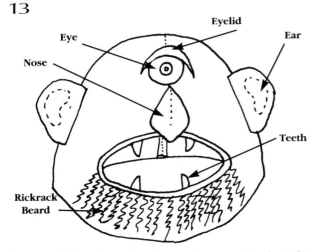

❖ Pin eyelid and eye in place as shown. Hand stitch in place.

❖ Repeat for ears, then nose, then teeth.

14

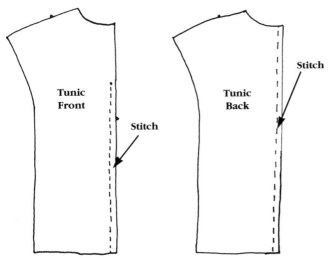

❖ Right sides together, pin and stitch two tunic pieces together, leaving opening above circle. Press seam open.

❖ Right sides together, pin and stitch tunic center back seam. Press seam open.

15

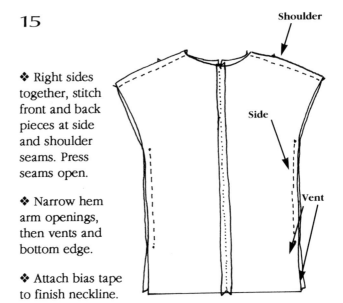

❖ Right sides together, stitch front and back pieces at side and shoulder seams. Press seams open.

❖ Narrow hem arm openings, then vents and bottom edge.

❖ Attach bias tape to finish neckline.

❖ Stitch shoulder pads to shoulder seams.

16

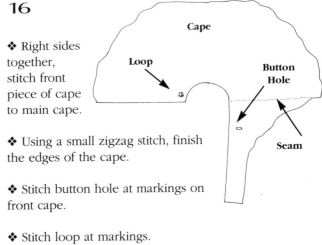

❖ Right sides together, stitch front piece of cape to main cape.

❖ Using a small zigzag stitch, finish the edges of the cape.

❖ Stitch button hole at markings on front cape.

❖ Stitch loop at markings.

❖ Insert chicken bone through loop to fasten.

17

❖ Cut two 3/8" x 30" (1 x 76 cm) strips of imitation leather for laces.

❖ Use laces to fasten legging to lower legs.

See Photo on page 71.

FABRIC

45" x 2-1/2 yd. (114.3 cm x 228.6 cm) Black fabric

Lots of scraps in different colors, fake fur, old panty hose, tights

NOTIONS

4 oz. Polyester fiberfill

ACCESSORIES

Gloves (see *Gorilla* costume)

Ovals of fake fur pinned onto shoes

Note: Hot glue can be substituted for sewing in this costume.

1

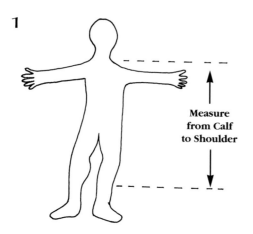

❖ Measure child from shoulder to calf. Cut two rectangles of black fabric 45" (114.3 cm) x this measurement.

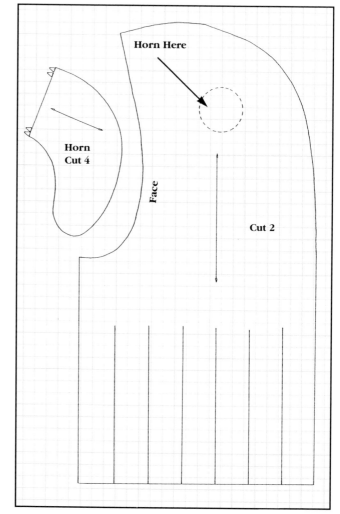

PATTERN SHOWN AT 25 % ACTUAL SIZE

2

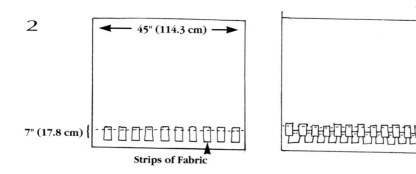
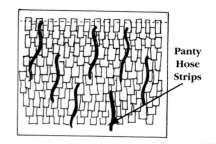

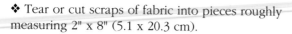

❖ Tear or cut scraps of fabric into pieces roughly measuring 2" x 8" (5.1 x 20.3 cm).

❖ To each rectangle sew these strips of cloth in rows. Start row at bottom of rectangle, approx. 7" (17.8 cm) from bottom edge. Continue stitching strips of fabric until rectangle is full. Glue or stitch additional strips of pantyhose, tights and fake fur.

3

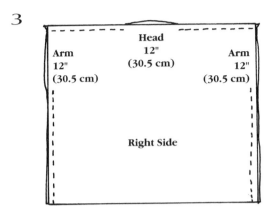

❖ Right sides facing out, pin and stitch the two rectangles together at shoulder seams and side seams, as shown. Leave a 12" (30.5 cm) opening for head and for arms. After trying costume on child, these openings may have to be adjusted for a better fit.

4

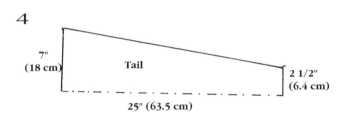

❖ Right sides together, fold tail in half, pin and stitch.

❖ Turn tail right side out and lightly stuff with polyester fiberfill.

❖ Glue small piece of fake fur to end of tail.

❖ Stitch tail to center back of costume.

5

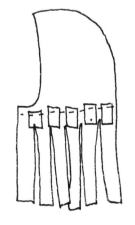

❖ Stitch strips of fabric to each half of headpiece as shown on costume body.

6

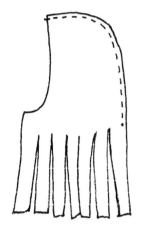

❖ Right sides together, stitch headpiece as shown.

7

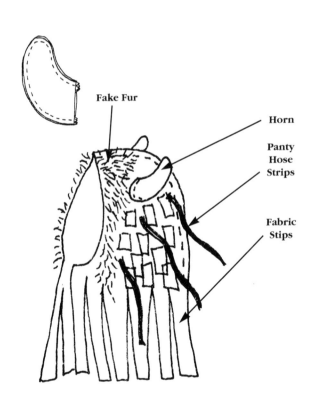

❖ Right sides together, pin two horn pieces together. Stitch, leave opening between double notches. Clip seams and turn right side out. Stuff firmly with polyester fiberfill. Turn under seam allowance. Hand stitch horns to headpiece as marked.

CHINESE DRAGON

See Photo on page 72.

FABRIC

   3 yds. (2.75 m) Red satin
   1-1/2 yd. (1.4 m) Gold lamé
   1-1/2 yd. (1.4 m) Iron-on interfacing

NOTIONS

   Newspapers
   Masking tape
   White glue
   Papier-mâché pulp
   Gesso
   Acrylic paint (gold, orange, black, green, white)
   Corrugated cardboard
   Gloss varnish (optional)
   Hot glue and gun

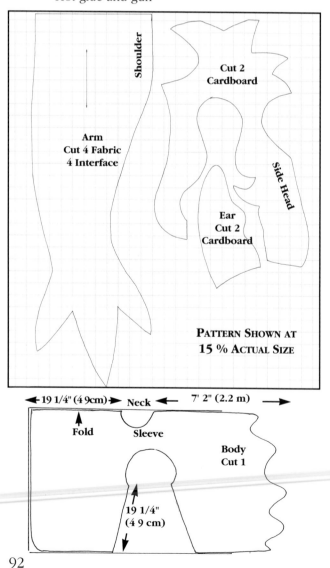

Arm
Cut 4 Fabric
4 Interface

Shoulder

Cut 2
Cardboard

Side Head

Ear
Cut 2
Cardboard

PATTERN SHOWN AT
15 % ACTUAL SIZE

◀ 19 1/4" (4 9cm) ▶ Neck ◀ 7' 2" (2.2 m) ▶

Fold ↑ Sleeve

Body
Cut 1

19 1/4"
(4 9 cm)

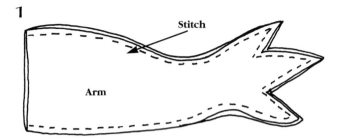

1

Stitch

Arm

❖ Apply iron-on interfacing to all arm pieces.

❖ Right sides together, pin two arm pieces together. Stitch, leaving opening as shown.

❖ Trim and clip seams. Turn right side out, press.

❖ Repeat for remaining pair of arms.

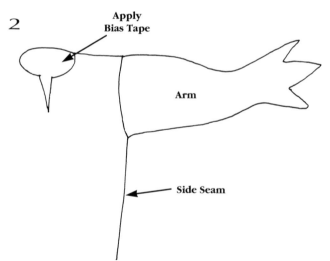

2

Apply
Bias Tape

Arm

Side Seam

❖ Right sides together, stitch arm to sleeve opening.

❖ Stitch side seam closed.

❖ Apply bias tape to front opening and neck edge.

❖ Apply iron-on interfacing to strips of gold lamé 2-1/2"–3" (6.5–7.5 cm) wide. Cut into scallops. Hot glue to costume front and sides.

3

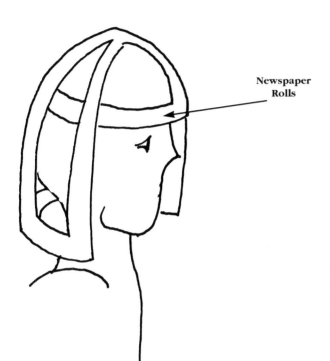

Newspaper
Rolls

❖ The dragon head is made from papier-mâché. Roll newspaper into several rolls and tape securely. Construct a helmet shape to fit head by taping the rolls of newspaper together.

❖ Cut side head from cardboard and hot glue in place on newspaper helmet.

❖ Round out the form by crumpling newspapers, placing them in the voids of the helmet, and taping them securely in place. Refer to the photo for shape.

❖ Check to make sure that the helmet has not been deformed and will still fit the child's head.

4

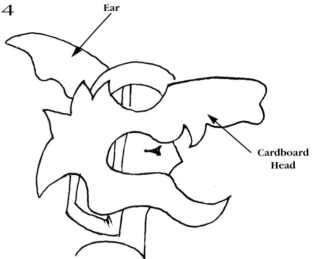

Ear

Cardboard
Head

❖ Cut or tear strips of newspaper approx. 1-2" (4 cm) wide. Dip strips into a mixture of 1/2 white glue and 1/2 water. Apply strips to the armature. Alternate the direction that you place the strips to avoid weak spots. Try to give even coverage to all surfaces.

❖ Allow to dry. Papier-mâché is slow drying. Turn the piece every day so that no mildew develops.

❖ After helmet is dry you can add detail to the project with papier-mâché pulp. Mix the pulp with water. Allow the pulp to sit in a plastic bag for 10 to 15 min. The pulp will act much like a clay. Add your details, such as teeth, eyelids, etc.

❖ Allow the helmet to dry thoroughly, turning it to prevent mildew.

5

❖ Apply gesso (acrylic primer) to helmet.

❖ Paint helmet (see photo).

❖ Applying gloss varnish will further strengthen the helmet and is recommended if you will be reusing the helmet over many years.

OUT OF THIS WORLD

PLANET EARTH

See instructions on page 106.

Waddya want, the world? You got it! Cast a big shadow and eclipse the competition at your next costume contest. At the least, you may teach some geography and raise a little eco-awareness.

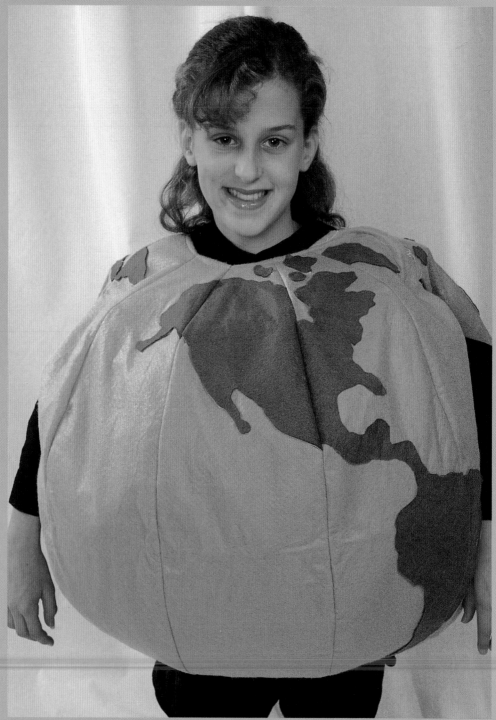

LUCKY LINDY

See instructions on page 108.

In 1927, Charles Lindbergh conquered the air by flying alone across the Atlantic in his monoplane, The Spirit of St. Louis. This costume may not fly, but it will give wings to the pioneer spirit in your child.

LITTLE ANGEL

See instructions on page 112.

Do angels really exist? If you have any doubts, dress up your own little cherub in this costume, and see if they can act as well as look the part. (No money-back guarantee on this one.)

WISHING STAR

See instructions on page 114.

"Twinkle, twinkle, little star, how I wonder what you are…" The birth of a star is a very complicated process that astronomers are only beginning to understand. So make a wish, who knows, maybe your child has star potential.

ROCK STAR

See instructions on page 116.

In the world of entertainment, image is everything. So what could be more superficial than putting on the glitz with this phony foam rubber facade?

SPACE CADET

See instructions on page 118.

When your child gets that far away look in their eyes, they're probably ready for a fantasy vacation. Send them to another galaxy for some R & R (Rascals & Revelry) in this versatile costume.

TWO-HEADED ALIEN

See instructions on page 120.

We really don't know where this guy (these guys?) came from. Mars, Neptune, some distant galaxy? What matters is whether pairs of Earth children will want to impersonate him (her, them…it's so confusing).

CAPTAIN GADGET

See instructions on page 122.

Anything that moves, makes noise, or really works can be incorporated into this inventive, free-form creation. Here is a young gadgeteer's dream come true.

THE MACHINE

See instructions on page 123.

Kids are quick to pick up on the love affair between man and machine that has existed since the invention of the wheel. Let your child try on this apparatus, and watch it come to life.

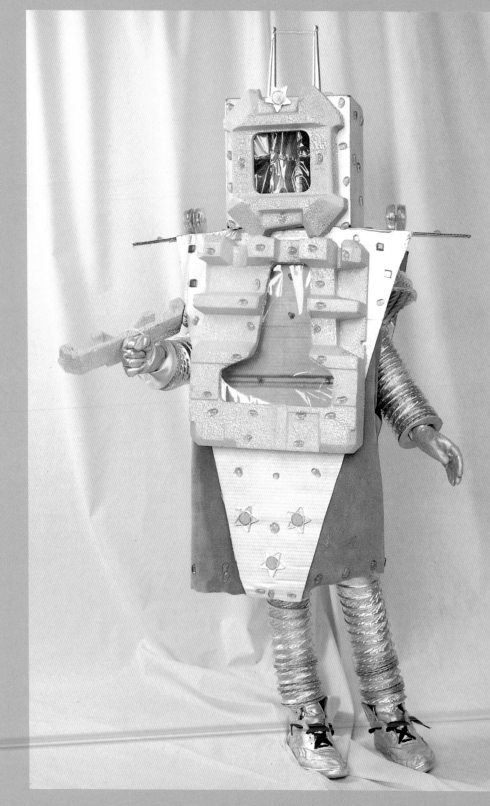

No. 2 Pencil

See instructions on page 125.

If "But teacher, I swallowed my pencil" was little Johnny's No. 1 excuse for not doing his homework, here is No. 2. Still not impressed? No. 3, "The dog ate it."

Blast Off

See instructions on page 126.

To boldly go, where no pencil has gone before…If your child exhibits escapist tendencies, they'll go ballistic over this design.

Self Portrait

See instructions on opposite page.

Ever thought of yourself as a walking work of art? This costume gives you artistic license to answer the question: can we ever see ourselves as others see us?

Self Portrait

See Photo on opposite page.

Materials

　　21" x 26" (53 x 66 cm) Foam core insulation
　　　board
　　11" x 12" x 16" (28 x 30.5 x 40 cm) Corrugated
　　　cardboard box
　　11" x 16" (28 x 40 cm) White mat board
　　Spray paints (flat black, gold)
　　Acrylic hobby paints
　　White glue

1

❖ Open the flaps on one large side of the box and cut them to 1" (2.5 cm). Glue the side flaps to the end flaps to form a flat edge around the open side of the box. Cut a circle 8" (20 cm) in diameter from one end of the box. Spray the outside of the box with black paint.

2

❖ For a portrait frame, cut a rectangle 20" x 30" (51 x 76 cm) from the foam board. Cut a rectangular whole approximately 9" x 13" (23 x 33 cm) from the center of the frame. If desired, cut decorative notches around the edges of the frame and glue strips of foam board onto the front. Spray the frame with gold paint.

3

❖ Cut a rectangle of white cardboard about 1" (2.5 cm) larger all around than the opening in the frame. Have the child put on the box. Tape the cardboard behind the frame, and hold the frame against the box to determine placement for the face cutout. Remove the cardboard from the frame, cut out the face area, and paint the hair.

4

❖ For a full portrait, make a longer frame and cut white cardboard to fit. Mark position for the face cutout as before, and paint the figure on the cardboard. You can have fun deciding what sort of figure to portray, whether an old masterpiece, a contemporary celebrity, or a caricature of yourself. Shoulder straps can be added to the back of the frame for more support.

5

❖ Glue the painted cardboard portrait to the back of the frame. Glue the frame to the flaps of the box.

See Photo on page 94.

FABRIC

> 1-1/4 yd. (114 cm) Blue felt
> 1 yd. (91 cm) Green felt
> 2 yds. (183 cm) Heavyweight iron-on
>   interfacing
> 1 yd. (91 cm) Fusible web

NOTIONS

> 2 yds. (183 cm) Bias tape
> 4 yds. (3.7 m) Boning
> Hot glue and gun

❖ Apply iron-on interfacing to the 12 blue sections.

❖ Appliqué with fusible web the green earth shapes.

❖ Right sides together, pin and stitch sections together sequentially.

❖ Leave arm openings between section 6 and 7 and section 11 and 12. Stitch 5-1/2" (14 cm) from top, then leave an opening 8-1/4" (21 cm) for arm.

❖ Apply bias tape to ends.

❖ On the inside, glue boning around the center, 1/2 of the way from center and the top, and 1/2 from center and the bottom.

❖ After putting on the costume, the inside can be stuffed with wadded newspaper to help keep its shape.

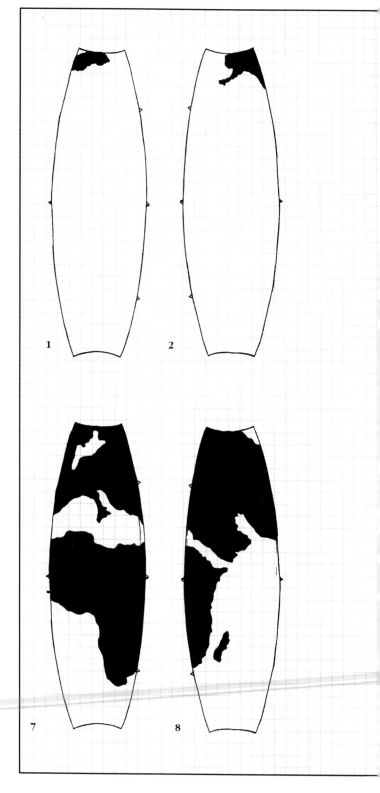

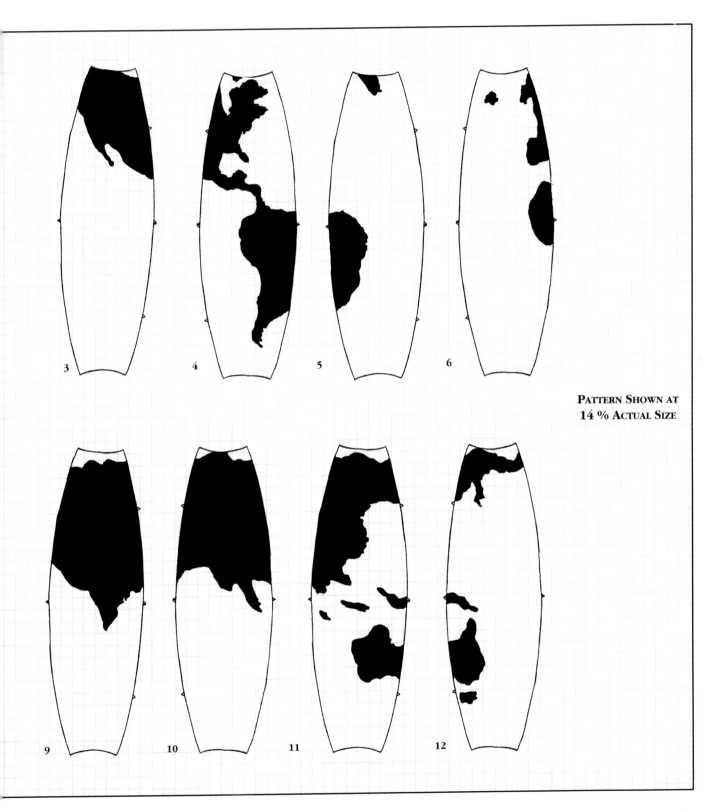

3

4

5

6

**PATTERN SHOWN AT
14 % ACTUAL SIZE**

9

10

11

12

See Photo on page 95.

FABRIC

- 1/4 yd. (23 cm) Brown imitation leather
- 1/4 yd. (23 cm) Fake fur
- 1/8 yd. (11.4 cm) Buckram or heavy interfacing

NOTIONS

- #16 Sewing machine needle
- 36" x 48" (0.9 x 1.2 m) Corrugated cardboard
- Bottom of 2 liter soda bottle
- 2 Cardboard tubes from paper towels
- 2 Washers
- Nut and bolt

- Webbing
- Hot glue and gun
- Chrome spray paint

ACCESSORIES

- Leather flight jacket and scarf
- Knickers and boots
- Goggles

SEAM ALLOWANCE

- 1/2" (1.3 cm)

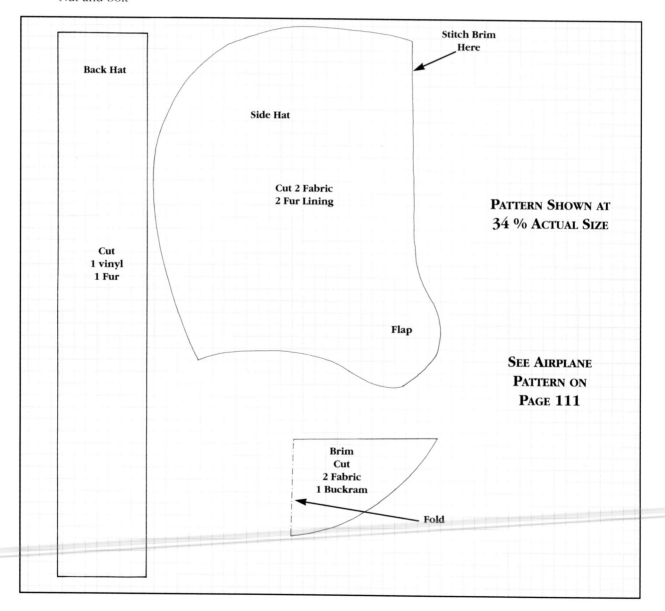

Back Hat

Stitch Brim Here

Side Hat

Cut 2 Fabric
2 Fur Lining

Cut
1 vinyl
1 Fur

PATTERN SHOWN AT
34 % ACTUAL SIZE

Flap

SEE AIRPLANE
PATTERN ON
PAGE 111

Brim
Cut
2 Fabric
1 Buckram

Fold

1

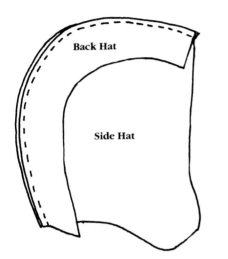

❖ Right sides together, pin and stitch back hat to side hat.

❖ Repeat for remaining side of hat to back of hat.

❖ Topstitch 1/4" (6 mm) from each side of seams.

❖ Repeat for lining. Omit topstitching.

2

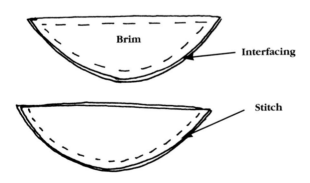

❖ Baste buckram to wrong side of leather brim.

❖ Right sides together, stitch brim and brim lining together.

❖ Trim seams and turn right side out.

❖ Edgestitch and topstitch along finished brim.

3

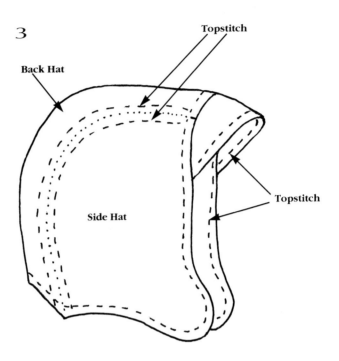

❖ Right sides together, pin and baste brim to hat.

❖ Right sides together, pin and stitch lining to hat. Leave an opening at back neck edge for turning. Trim and clip seams. Turn hat right side out. Edgestitch and topstitch outside edge of hat, same as brim.

4

❖ Using a craft knife, cut pieces from corrugated cardboard.

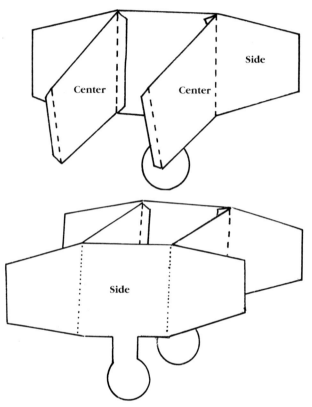

❖ Hot glue center pieces to right and left side pieces.

5

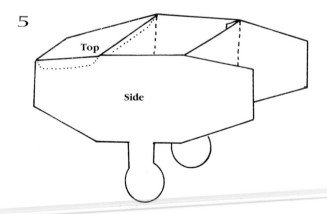

❖ Glue top front and top back pieces to center and side.

6

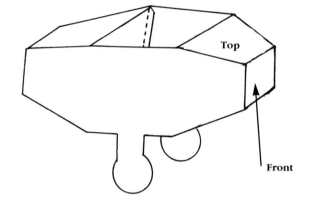

❖ Glue front and back pieces.

7

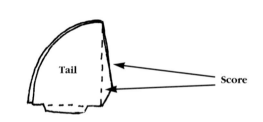

❖ Score tail along dotted lines. Glue tail together along curved edge.

8

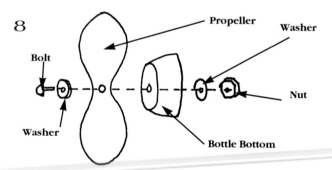

❖ Attach cut-out propeller to the bottom of a 2 liter plastic soda bottle.

❖ Glue soda bottle bottom to center front of airplane.

9

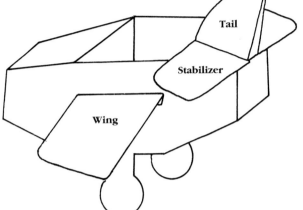

❖ Cut slot for tail in center back of airplane. Glue tail.

❖ Glue stabilizers.

❖ Glue wings to side body of plane. Using cardboard tubes, angle-cut diagonal struts to fit under the wings, and attach to side body of the plane. Glue.

❖ Cut two slits in front and two slits in back of plane for harness. This harness will hold the plane on the child's shoulders.

❖ Thread webbing from back to front. Adjust length to fit child.

❖ Spray paint the airplane.

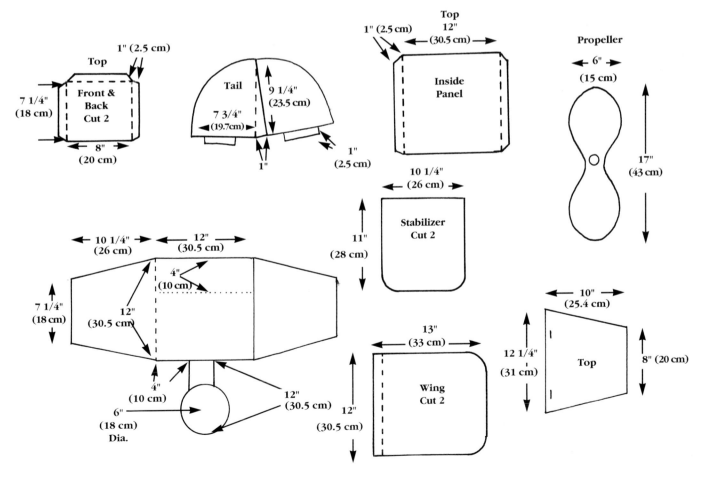

See Photo on page 96.

FABRIC

26" x 18" (66 cm x 45.7 cm) White satin
36" x 18" (91.4 cm x 45.7 cm) Gold lamé with
knit backing
26" x 9" (66 cm x 22.9 cm) Polyester fiberfill
batting

NOTIONS

2 oz. Loose polyester fiberfill
36" of 1/2" (91.4 of 1.3 cm) Elastic
18" x 18" (45.7 x 45.7 cm) Cardboard or
Buckram
18" x 18" of 1/2" (47.5 x 47.5 of 1.3 cm) Foam
sheeting

ACCESSORIES

Long nightgown or nightshirt (or use *Merlin's*
pattern)
Sandals or slippers

Cut 2 Fabric
1 Batting

PATTERN SHOWN AT
25 % ACTUAL SIZE

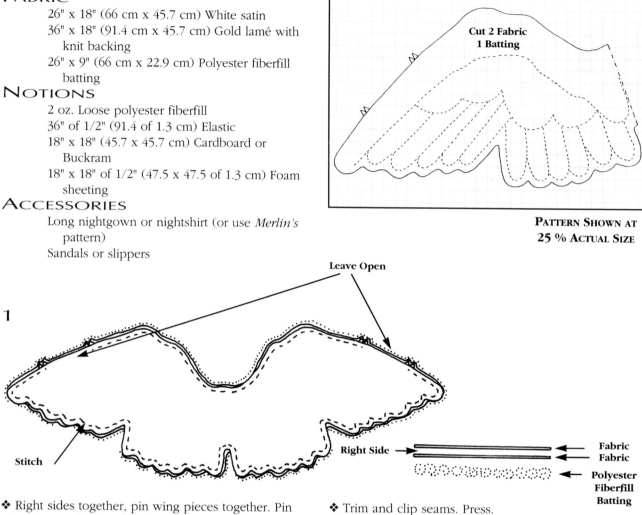

Leave Open

1

Stitch

Right Side →

Fabric
Fabric

Polyester
Fiberfill
Batting

❖ Right sides together, pin wing pieces together. Pin wings to matching piece of polyester fiberfill batting. Stitch. Leave open between double notches for turning and stuffing.

❖ Trim and clip seams. Press.

2

Stuff Here

Machine Quilt

❖ Machine quilt wings along dotted lines.

❖ Stuff polyester fiberfill into top of wings through openings between double notches. Fill entire shaded space. This will stiffen wings. Pin and turn seam allowances of opening to inside, baste closed.

❖ Hand stitch openings closed.

3

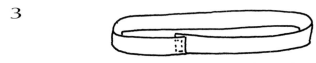

❖ Lap ends of elastic 1/2" (1.3 cm) and stitch together.

4

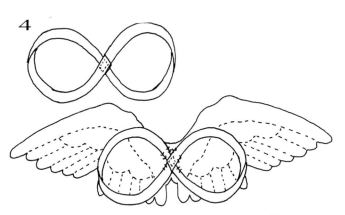

❖ Form elastic into a figure 8. Pin to center of wings as shown.

❖ Hand stitch elastic to wings.

5

Head Dia. +1" (2.6 cm)

3" (7.6 cm)

1/4" (6mm)
Seam Allowance

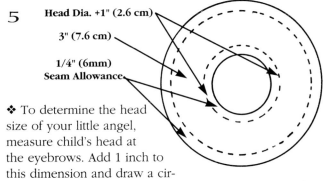

❖ To determine the head size of your little angel, measure child's head at the eyebrows. Add 1 inch to this dimension and draw a circle. Add 3 inches (7.6 cm) to the head dimension and draw a second concentric circle. Draw a 1/4" (6 mm) seam allowance for inside and outside of circle.

❖ The interior circle will be the same as the diameter of your child's head, plus 1 inch (2.5 cm). Use this pattern to cut 2 pieces of gold lamé. Then remove all seam allowances from the pattern and cut 1 piece of cardboard and 1 piece of foam.

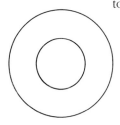

6

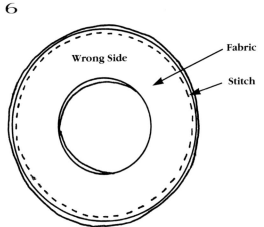

Wrong Side

Fabric

Stitch

❖ Right sides together, pin fabric circles together. Stitch outside circle. Clip seams. Turn and press.

❖ Insert cardboard between fabric circles. Insert foam between cardboard and fabric circles. (You will have to fold the cardboard and foam to insert into the fabric casing.) Baste opening closed.

7

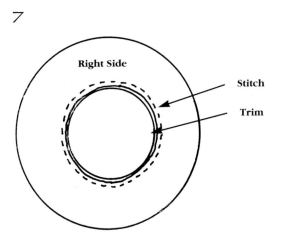

Right Side

Stitch

Trim

❖ Use a zipper foot on your sewing machine. Stitch inside circle of halo. Trim seam to 1/8" (3 mm). *Note:* Lamé (knit backed) does not fray. Do not worry about raw edge. It will be hidden by child's hair when costume is worn.

See Photo on page 97.

FABRIC

1 yd. (91.4 cm) Gold lamé, knit backing
1/2 yd. (45.7 cm) Lining

NOTIONS

20" x 20" of 1/2" (51 x 51 of 1.3 cm) Foam
    rubber
1 oz. Polyester fiberfill stuffing
12" x 1/4" (30.5 x 0.6 cm) Wooden dowel
Gold paint
1 yd. of 1/4" (91.4 of 0.6 cm) Ribbons

ACCESSORIES

White leotard and tights
Ballerina's tutu and slippers

SEAM ALLOWANCE

1/2" (1.3 cm)

1

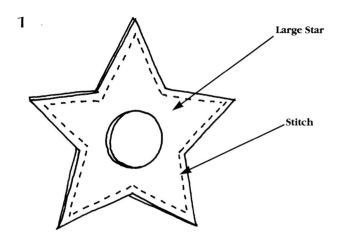

❖ Right sides together, pin large star together, stitch as shown. Clip seams and turn. Press.

❖ Insert matching foam shape through face opening. Baste opening closed.

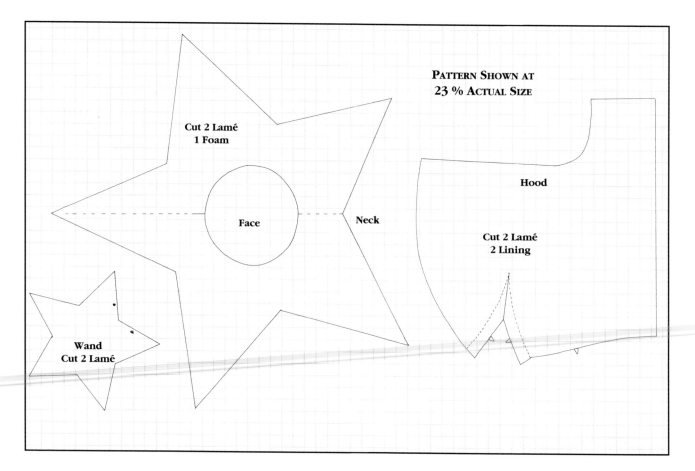

2

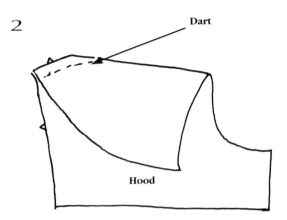

Dart

Hood

❖ Right sides together, matching notches and stitching line, pin and stitch dart on hood and hood lining.

3

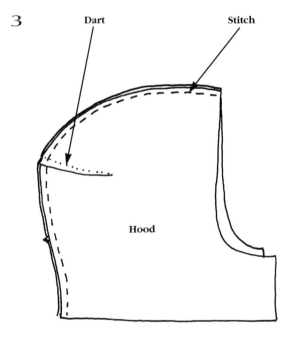

Dart

Stitch

Hood

❖ Right sides together, pin center back seam on hood together, stitch. Repeat for lining.

❖ Right sides together, pin lining to hood leaving face area open. Stitch, clip and trim seams. Turn right side out. Baste lining to hood at open seam.

4

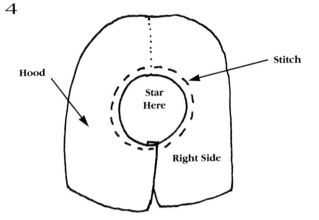

Hood

Stitch

Star Here

Right Side

❖ Place large star next to lining on hood. Matching center seam, pin hood opening to large star, overlap hood at center front. Baste. Stitch. Clip seam and overcast raw edges. Turn star to outside. Seam will now be between the large star and hood.

5

Leave Open

❖ Right sides together, pin and stitch small star shape, leave opening between double notches. Clip seams, turn. Stuff.

❖ Paint wooden dowel with gold paint. When paint is dry insert dowel into opening in small star. Hot glue star onto dowel. Decorate joint with ribbons.

See Photo on page 98.

MATERIALS

5' x 6' x 1/2" (153 x 183 x 1.3 cm) Foam
    rubber, or other size to fit child
Two 4" (10 cm) Foam rubber balls
Single strand sequins: 4 yds. (3.7 m) Pink
               4 yds. (3.7 m) Purple
               5-1/2 yds. (5 m) Green
1/2 yd. of 3/4" (46 of 2 cm) Pink sequin
    braid belt
Three strips of 7" x 1 yd. (18 x 91 cm) Lace
    of metallic fabric for hair
Five assorted plastic gems
Glitter (gold, silver, multi-color)
Spray paint (gold)
Acrylic paint (red, blue)
White glue
Foam adhesive
Hot glue and gun

PATTERN

❖ Trace outline of child, lying down, onto a large sheet of paper—or directly onto the foam rubber. Construct a star pattern that conforms to the child's proportions (see drawing).

❖ Mark the opening for the face from eyebrow to upper lip. Draw in remaining features of the star's face and body. If you want to vary the design of the outfit, experiment on paper first.

CUT

❖ Cut out the star with a sharp utility knife or razor blade. Cut the opening for the face.

❖ Cut a triangle the same size as the top point of the star. This will be attached later to form a pocket for the head.

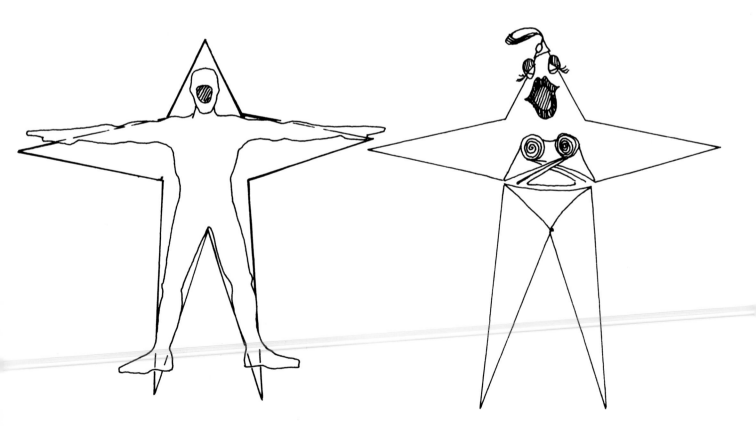

❖ Cut foam for lips and shape them. Cut one foam ball in half for the breasts. Cut the other foam ball in quarters for eyelids.

ASSEMBLE

❖ Apply foam adhesive to both surfaces of top edges of triangle, and attach to top of star body to form head pocket. Follow instructions on can for best results.

❖ Glue breast pieces to body. Eyes and lips will be attached later after painting.

PAINT

❖ Spray the body gold. Yellow can also be used as a base cut to brighten the gold.

❖ Using acrylics, paint the lips red and the pupils of the eyes blue. Allow them to dry thoroughly.

DECORATE

❖ To apply glitter, dilute 1/2 cup white glue with 1-2 tablespoons of water and apply with a brush. Sprinkle glitter over glue and let dry. Shake excess away before applying the next color.

❖ Sequins, gems, fabric, beads and other trimmings can be attached to the body using a hot glue gun. Refer to the photo for finishing details, or decorate as you please. The key word is "glitz."

❖ Glamorous eyelashes can be fashioned out of pipe cleaners and hot glued onto outer corners of eyelids. A variation for eyelashes would be plastic beads strung on wires and glued in place.

STRAPS

❖ To attach straps, see instructions for *Gingerbread Man*.

GUITAR

❖ You'll probably want to accessorize with an electric guitar, if you have one. Or, with a little imagination and effort, you can make a stylized guitar like the one in the photo. This guitar was improvised using a picture frame for the body, a reinforced long glove for the neck, and jazzed up with all sorts of decorative materials including a pair of tiny sneakers.

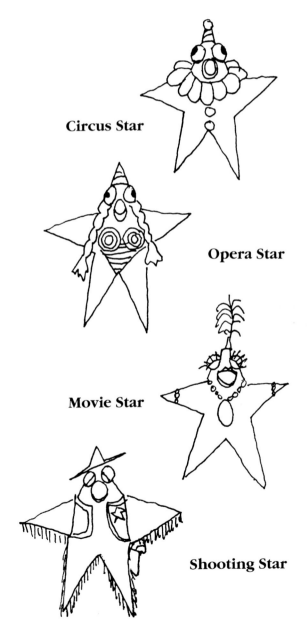

Circus Star

Opera Star

Movie Star

Shooting Star

117

SPACE CADET

See Photo on page 99.

FABRIC

   5/8 yd. (57.2 cm) Metallic fabric
   1 yd. (91.4 cm) Taffeta
   5/8 yd. (57.2 cm) Quilted fabric

NOTIONS

   7" of 1/2" (18 of 1.3 cm) Elastic

SEAM ALLOWANCE

   1/2" (1.3 cm)

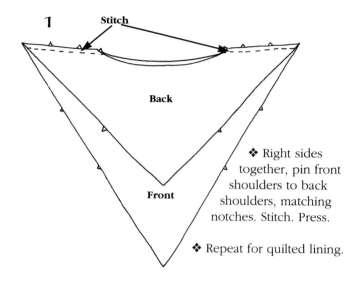

❖ Right sides together, pin front shoulders to back shoulders, matching notches. Stitch. Press.

❖ Repeat for quilted lining.

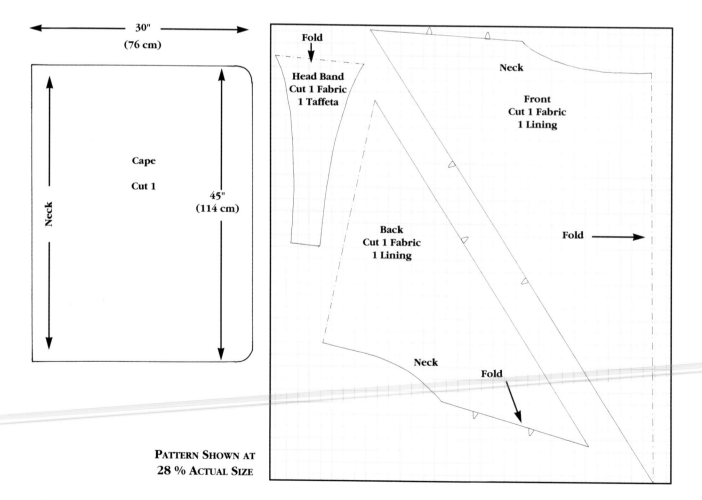

PATTERN SHOWN AT 28 % ACTUAL SIZE

2

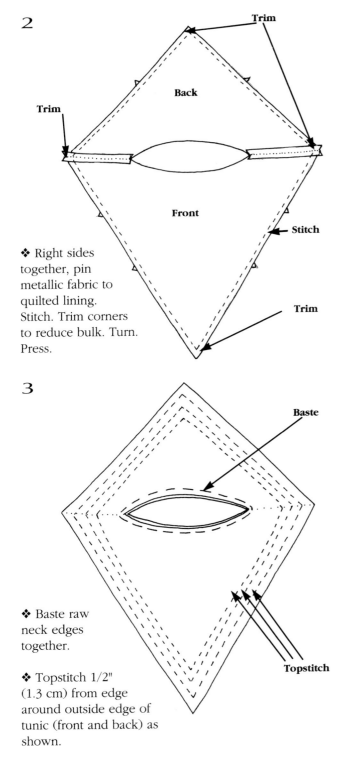

Trim

Trim

Back

Trim

Front

Stitch

Trim

❖ Right sides together, pin metallic fabric to quilted lining. Stitch. Trim corners to reduce bulk. Turn. Press.

3

Baste

Topstitch

❖ Baste raw neck edges together.

❖ Topstitch 1/2" (1.3 cm) from edge around outside edge of tunic (front and back) as shown.

4

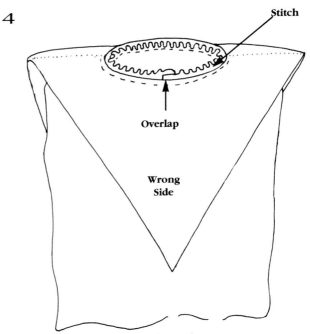

Stitch

Overlap

Wrong Side

❖ Finish side and bottom edges of cape.

❖ Gather neck edge of cape.

❖ Right sides together, pin neck edge of cape to neck opening in tunic. Overlap front of cape at center front 3/4" (1.9 cm). Adjust gathers in cape evenly. Stitch.

❖ Press seam toward cape.

❖ Zigzag stitch cape to seam.

5

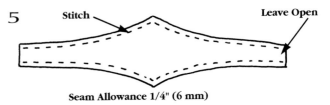

Stitch

Leave Open

Seam Allowance 1/4" (6 mm)

❖ Right sides together, pin headband pieces together. Stitch, leaving ends open. Clip seams. Turn, press.

❖ Measure child's head. Cut elastic to fit. Stitch elastic to headband.

TWO-HEADED ALIEN

See Photo on page 100.

FABRIC

3-3/4 yds. of 45" wide (3.4 m of 114 cm)
Greenish crinkly polyester

NOTIONS

Loose pack of fiberfill
Styrofoam packing chips
1 package of Silver braid trim, or any silver
fabric cut into four 3' (.9 m) strips
4 Shoulder pads, 1" thick

1

❖ Double the fabric, lengthwise, wrong side out. On the mask, the marked lines are stitching lines. Cut around outer edges of the mask, head top, and ear pieces, adding about 1/4" (6 mm) for seam allowance around the outer edges, but cutting the lower edges on the marked lines. Cut the sleeve without adding seam allowance. Mark all notches as shown on the pattern pieces.

2

❖ Sew the mask pieces together in pairs. Stitch on marked lines and leave open in back below the notch at the placement line.

❖ Sew the head top pieces together in some way, leaving an opening at the back between notches.

❖ Turn the masks and head tops right side out and press seams. Use a rolled towel to press the curves. Mark placement lines for head tops on the right sides of the masks. Stitch head tops in place, using a zigzag stitch to overcast the raw edge at the same time.

❖ Stitch the ears together in pairs, leaving lower edges open. Turn right side out and stuff loosely with fiberfill. Machine stitch to quilt the ears, as shown on the pattern piece, and stitch closed across lower edges. Stitch the ears onto the masks.

❖ Stuff the head tops loosely with styrofoam chips or fiberfill. Stitch the openings closed.

❖ Try the masks on the children and mark placement of eyes, nostrils, and mouths. Cut openings.

❖ Paint details on the masks using the photo as a guide—or let the children paint them, using their imagination.

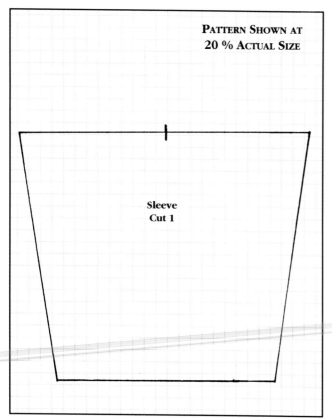

PATTERN SHOWN AT 20 % ACTUAL SIZE

**Sleeve
Cut 1**

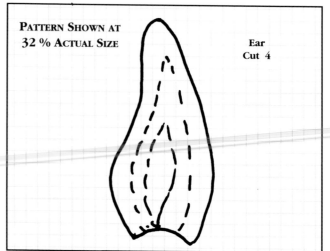

PATTERN SHOWN AT 32 % ACTUAL SIZE

**Ear
Cut 4**

3

❖ For the tunic, fold the remaining fabric in half, crosswise, right side out, and trim the raw edges evenly.

❖ Mark a point on the fold at each selvedge edge for the shoulder. From one side, mark a point on the fold 12" (30.5 cm) in from the edge, then make another mark 6" (15.2 cm) in from the first. Halfway between these marks draw a line 2-1/2" (6.4 cm) long, perpendicular to the fold. Draw a semicircle between the two marks, with the rounded edge extending to the bottom of the line. Cut out the semicircle for the front neckline. At the center of the back neckline, cut a 6" (15.2 cm) slit perpendicular to the fold. Make the second neckline in the same way, measuring from the other selvedge edge.

❖ Right sides together, pin a sleeve to each side, matching the notch at the sleeve top to the mark at the shoulder. Stitch, using 1/2" (1.3 cm) seam allowance. Press the seams toward the sleeves. Sew the sides and under sleeves.

❖ Hem the bottom of the tunic and sleeves, if desired, and finish neck edges with a zigzag stitch. Tape or stitch shoulder pads in place—2 on each outer shoulder.

❖ With the tunic on the children, tie silver strips around the arms.

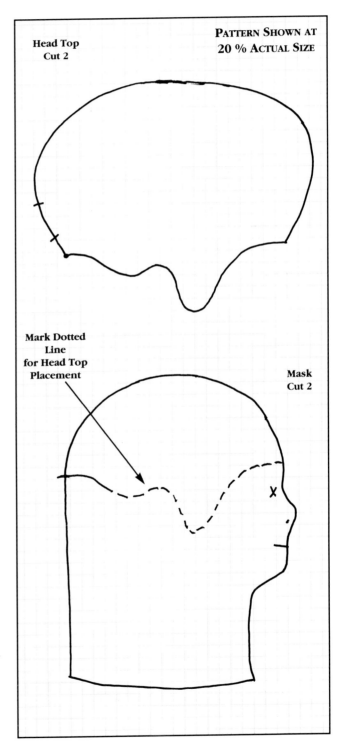

Head Top
Cut 2

PATTERN SHOWN AT
20 % ACTUAL SIZE

Mark Dotted
Line
for Head Top
Placement

Mask
Cut 2

Captian Gadget

See Photo on page 101.

Materials

An old coat, hat, high-top sneakers
Fancy eyeglasses (e.g. with rear-view mirrors)
Colorful fine line fabric paints
Metallic fabric paint
Spray paints
Enamel hobby paints
Mylar sheet (a.k.a. energy blanket for camping)
Thin wire
Fishing line
Assorted paper clips
Small plastic beads
Sequins
Small model airplane propeller(s)
Duct tape
Tacky glue
Hot glue and gun
Lots of gadgets

First, you and your child can have a lot of fun going on "gadget treasure hunts." Let your imagination run wild in hardware stores, hobby shops, camping outfitters, bike and auto suppliers, toy stores, office supply stores, rummage sales—even your own basement, closets and garage. There are various ways to construct the costume, but here are some guidelines that worked for us.

1

❖ Eyeglasses can be decorated, painted, or fitted with attachable shades or rear-view mirrors (from a bicycle shop).

2

❖ Shoes can be spray painted, then designs added afterwards with fabric paints and glue-on items. Mylar fans can be sewn on at the ankles. These are made by cutting a rectangle of mylar about 6" x 8" (15 x 20 cm) and folding it up accordion-style. Staple it across one end, then fan it out.

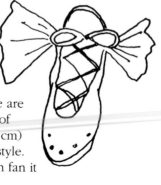

3

❖ Any sort of hat, cap or helmet can be painted and decorated with glue-on items, mylar fringe, and functioning attachments. For a propeller, cut a length of wire about 6" (15 cm), twist one end into 4 small petal shapes to form a flat base. Cut a hole through the top of the hat, insert the wire up through it, and secure petals to inside with duct tape. String a few beads down the wire shaft, then the propeller, then a couple more beads, and twist the wire over the top bead.

4

❖ The coat can be painted all sorts of ways. Focus on pockets, collars, and coordinate with the gadgets and other decorations you'll be adding. Mylar fans can be sewn onto shoulders. Fringe can be added around shoulders and the coat's bottom edge. All the gadgets and decorative items can be arranged for visual effect and/or to be within reach of the child. Smaller, non-functioning items can be glued or sewn in place. Working gadgets should be attached so that they are still functional, perhaps with fishing line, or left dangling and accessible.

5

❖ A personalized super-hero logo would be an appropriate feature to add. Also, this costume may go through a gradual metamorphosis as your child's interests change and new gadgets are added on or replacing old ones. You may want to further accessorize with a belt pouch, back pack, brief case, tool box, tool belt and holsters, secret compartments, or hand held instruments.

See Photo on page 102.

MATERIALS

Corrugated cardboard sheets and box
Sections of styrofoam packing
Any heavy cloth
Large colored beads
Floral wire
Plastic party horns
Light-up yo-yos
Jumbo L.E.D.s
2 AA Batteries
Electrical speaker wire
Rubber gloves
Dryer vent hose
Colored cellophane paper
Silver spray paint
Bicycle reflectors
Two-part 5-minute epoxy glue
Hot glue and gun
Duct tape

This costume can be constructed in any number of ways using variations of design and materials. The important thing is to have fun and be as extravagant as you like.

Lighting notes: Up to 8 L.E.D.s can be powered by 2 AA batteries. They can be positioned elsewhere, like inside styrofoam sections with cellophane windows, or next to colored beads. All wire connections can be twisted together and/or soldered. Certain commercially available solders can even be melted with a match. Connections can be wrapped with tape so as not to prick any nearby skin. The circuit is switched off by removing the batteries. There is no danger of electrical shock from this system.

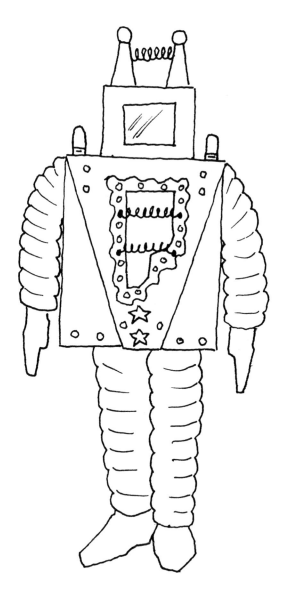

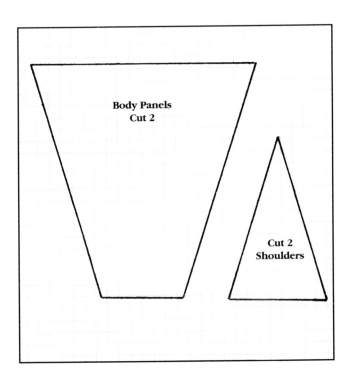

Body Panels
Cut 2

Cut 2
Shoulders

1

❖ Reshape and spray paint all styrofoam pieces.

2

❖ Cut out cardboard pieces for body and shoulders. Hot glue body panels together at shoulders. Hot glue body panels together at shoulders. Use cardboard box for head, cutting out ear holes for ventilation and face hole. Spray paint all cardboard. Cover face hole with cellophane, taped to inside.

3

❖ Cut side panels of heavy cloth. Spray paint if necessary. Hot glue to cardboard body panels.

4

❖ Epoxy cellophane sheets over any holes in the prepainted styrofoam pieces. Epoxy colored beads and bicycle reflectors onto these pieces in a hi-tech style.

5

❖ Cut sections of flexible vent hose for arms and legs. Spray paint them, along with rubber gloves and any footwear that will be used. Attach gloves to arm sections with duct tape.

6

❖ Attach speaker wire to L.E.D.s long enough to reach battery compartment which can be positioned anywhere on cardboard body panels. Attach L.E.D.s to tips of party horns and run wires through holes in top of head box before gluing in place. Wrap floral wire around a shaft (e.g. chair leg) to make a coil, then hot glue it between the party horns.

7

❖ Make or borrow a battery compartment for 2 size AA batteries from an old toy. Attach speaker wires and glue the compartment to body.

8

❖ Hot glue yo-yos to shoulders after attaching speaker wires. Cut the wires on either side of the switch inside the yo-yo and join them together. Connect to batteries.

9

❖ Glue the styrofoam sections to cardboard body panels with epoxy. Hot glue more beads and reflectors around body.

10

❖ Put on arm and leg pieces first, safety pinning them to shoulders and thighs of undergarments. Then place body assembly and head over the child, insert batteries, and off it goes.

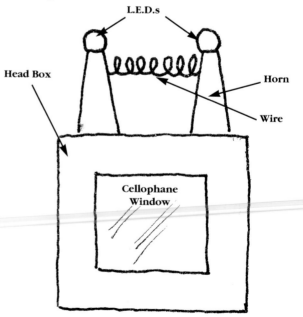

No. 2 Pencil

See Photo on page 103.

Fabric

16" x 45" (41 x 114 cm) Pink poly/cotton
9-1/2" x 45" (24 x 114 cm) Silver lamé
9-1/2" x 45" (24 x 114 cm) Lining
35" x 45" (89 x 114 cm) Yellow poly/cotton
1 yd. (0.9 m) Polyester fiberfill batting
2 yds. (1.8 m) Yellow bias tape
12" x 12" (30 x 30 cm) Black felt
36" x 20" (91 x 51 cm) Beige poly/cotton

Notions

Poster board (cone)
Corrugated cardboard (hexagon)
20" (51 cm) Webbing
Hot glue and gun

1

❖ Cut the following:

16" x 45" Pink poly/cotton
9-1/2" x 45" Silver lamé
9-1/2" x 45" Lining
9-1/2" x 45" Polyester fiberfill batting
35" x 45" Yellow poly/cotton

❖ Use patterns for additional pieces.

PATTERN SHOWN AT 11 % ACTUAL SIZE

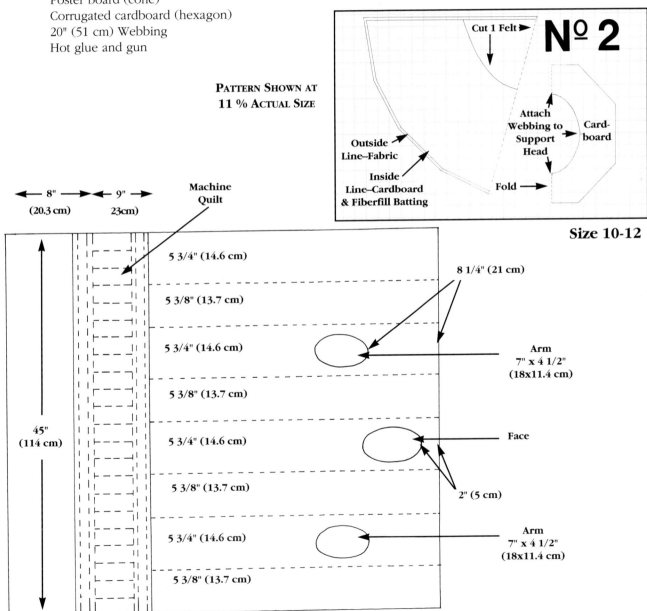

2

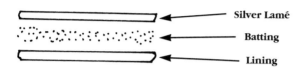

Silver Lamé

Batting

Lining

❖ Make a sandwich of silver lamé, polyester fiberfill batting and lining.

❖ Machine quilt using black thread as shown on pattern diagram.

3

❖ Fold pink fabric in half. Baste raw edges together.

❖ Right sides together, pin and stitch silver lamé to pink fabric. Press seams open.

❖ Using a small narrow zigzag stitch, sew as marked on yellow fabric. Use bias tape to finish edges of face and arm holes.

❖ Right sides together, stitch base of yellow fabric to silver lamé.

4

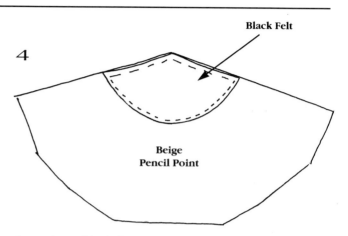

Black Felt

Beige
Pencil Point

❖ Appliqué black felt to pencil point.

5

❖ Right sides together, stitch beige pencil point to yellow fabric.

❖ Right sides together, stitch center back seam together. Stop stitching 20" (51 cm) from bottom.

6

❖ Hot glue cardboard cone to hexagon head piece.

❖ Cut two pieces of webbing and glue to marks on hexagon head piece.

❖ Glue polyester fiberfill batting to cardboard cone. Slip pencil covering over cone.

Blast Off

See Photo on page 103.

Notions

2' x 3' (61 x 91 cm) Corrugated cardboard
Silver spray paint

1

❖ Simply change the yellow and beige fabric in the *No. 2 Pencil* costume to silver, and the pink eraser to yellow flame, and substitute the NASA logo for No. 2.

2

❖ To make the fins, cut the cardboard rectangle diagonally in half and spray paint them silver. They can be hot glued, sewn or stapled to the fabric body. They can also be reinforced with 2 stiff cardboard hoops which are placed inside the fabric cylinder and attached to the fins at top and bottom.

BIBLIOGRAPHY

Papier-Mache Today
Sheila McGraw
Copyright 1990
Firefly Books Ltd.
250 Sparks Avenue
Willowdale, Ontario, Canada
M2H 2S4

Monsters and Ghouls, Costumes and Lore
Frieda Gates
Copyright 1980
Walker Publishing Company, Inc.
720 Fifth Avenue
New York, NY 10019

Costumes for You to Make
Susan Purdy
Copyright 1971
J. B. Lippincott Company
Philadelphia and New York

Masks
Lyndie Wright
Copyright 1990
Franklin Watts
387 Park Avenue South
New York, NY 10016

Party Costumes for Kids
Jean Greenhowe
Copyright 1988
Sterling Publishing Co., Inc.
2 Park Avenue
New York, NY 10016

Costumes from Crepe Paper
Marie-Blanche Pointillart
Copyright 1974
Sterling Publishing Co., Inc.
419 Park Avenue South
New York, NY 10016

Costumes to Make
Peggy Parish
Illustrated by Lynn Sweat
Copyright 1970
The MacMillan Company
866 Third Avenue
New York, NY 10022

Easy Costumes You Don't Have To Sew
Goldie Taub Chernoff
Costumes designed and illustrated by Margaret A. Hartelius
Copyright 1975
Four Winds Press
Scholastic Magazines, Inc.
New York, NY

The First Book of Stage Costume and Make-Up
Barbara Berk
Illustrated by Jeanne Bendic
Copyright 1954
Franklin Watts
New York, NY

Sewing Sculpture
Charleen Kinser
Copyright 1977
M Evans and Company, Inc.
New York, NY 10017

Patterns for Theatrical Costumes
Copyright 1984
Katherine Strand Holkeboer
Prentice Hall, Inc.
New Jersey

The No-Sew Costume Book
Michaeline Bresnahan
& Joan Gaestel Macfarlane
Copyright 1990
The Stephen Greene Press/Pelham Books
Penguin Books
New York

Story Telling with Puppets
ALA
Copyright 1985
Champlin and Renfro

Stage Costumes and How to Make Them
Julia Tompkins
Copyright 1968
Plays, Inc.
Boston, Mass.

101 Costumes for All Ages, All Occasions
Richard Cummings
ill. Opal Jackson
Copyright 1970
David McKay Company, Inc.
New York

Representing Children's Book Characters
Mary E. Wilson
Copyright 1989
The Scarecrow Press, Inc.
Metuchen, NJ and London

Paper Masks and Puppets for Stories, Songs and Plays
Ron and Marsha Feller
The Arts Factory
P.O. Box 55547
Seattle, WA 98155

Jane Asher's Fancy Dress
Jane Asher
Copyright 1983
Salem House
47 Pelham Road
Salem, NH 03079

CREDITS

All costumes were designed and constructed by **Michelle Lipson**, except for the following: **Carol Parks**—The Refrigerator, Muscle Maniac, Self Portrait, Two-Headed Alien; **Beryl Goddard**—Junkfood Junkie, The Machine; **Susan Brown-Strauss**—Gingerbread Man's Revenge, Rock Star; **Pat Samuels**—Captain Gadget; **Kay Johnson**—Meals on Wheels.

We wish to thank C.A.T.S. (Carolina Artisans Thespian Society) of Asheville, NC for providing most of our models:

Evan Boswell (pages 12, 14), Ariel Claire (58, 66, 98), Laurel Durland (94, 104), Willy Durland (61, 71), Mark Eaton de Verges (39, 67, 69, 70, 95, 100), Charley Hupertz (10, 36), Max Hupertz (13, 99), Jordan Samuels (68, 99), Daniel Sherlin (102), Christy Sherlin (58), Ellen Smith (11, 16, 97), Ryan Smith (42, 66, 72, 100, 103), Stephen Smith (40, 41, 60), Claire Stanhope (12, 37), Cecelia Thomas (96), Mariah Thomas (15, 38, 59).

INDEX

A

Alien, Two-Headed	100, 120
Angel, Little	96, 112

B

Bat	36, 43
Butterfly	37, 43

C

Cadet, Space	99, 118
Captain Gadget	101, 122
cardboard	7, 64, 92, 105, 108, 123, 125
Cat, Jungle	41, 52
Cockroach, Dreaded	69, 81
Cyclops	70, 86

D

Dragon, Chinese	72, 92
Dragonslayer	13, 24

E

Earth	94, 106
Elephant	40, 50

F

Firebird	38, 45
fire retardant	9
foam rubber	8, 48, 52, 55, 63, 81, 86, 112, 114, 116

G

Gingerbread Man	60, 63
Gorilla	42, 55
Grapes, Sour	59, 62
grid	8

J

Jester, Court	15, 29
Junkie, Junkfood	58, 62

L

Lady in Waiting	11, 18
Lindy, Lucky	95, 108

M

Machine	102, 123
Maid Marian	12, 23
Majesty, His Royal	10, 17
make believe	6
makeup	9
Maniac, Muscle	68, 80
materials, alternative	7
, collecting	7
Meals on Wheels	58, 62
Merlin the Magician	14, 27
Monster, Bog	71, 90
Mummy	67, 78

P

papier-mâché	51, 92, 93
Pencil, No. 2	103, 125
Prankster, Pixie	16, 33

R

Refrigerator	61, 64
Robin Hood	12, 21

S

seam allowance	8
Self Portrait	104, 105
Star, Rock	98, 116
, Wishing	97, 114

T

Toad, Happy	39, 48

W

Warlock, Weird	66, 76
Witch, Wicked	66, 73